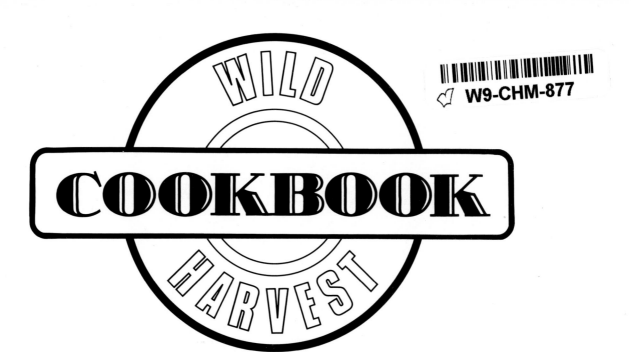

Dan Small and Nancy Frank
Photography by Daniel J. Cox

WILLOW CREEK

Second Edition
Text copyright © 1988 and © 1991 by Dan Small and Nancy Frank
Photographs © 1991 by Daniel J. Cox

OUTDOOR WISCONSIN is a production of WMVS-TV,
Milwaukee, a service of MATC.

ISBN 1-55971-113-2

Published by Willow Creek Press
An imprint of NorthWord Press, Inc.
Box 1360, Minocqua, WI 54548

For a free color catalog of other NorthWord products, call 1-800-336-5666.

Photo Credits

All photographs in Wild Harvest are by Daniel J. Cox except the following, which were provided by Dan Small: Pages 13, 85, 96, 117 and 121.
Cover photograph © Ed Hoppe, Boulder Junction, Wisconsin.

*This book is dedicated to all
who love the beauty and bounty
of the great outdoors.*

CONTENTS

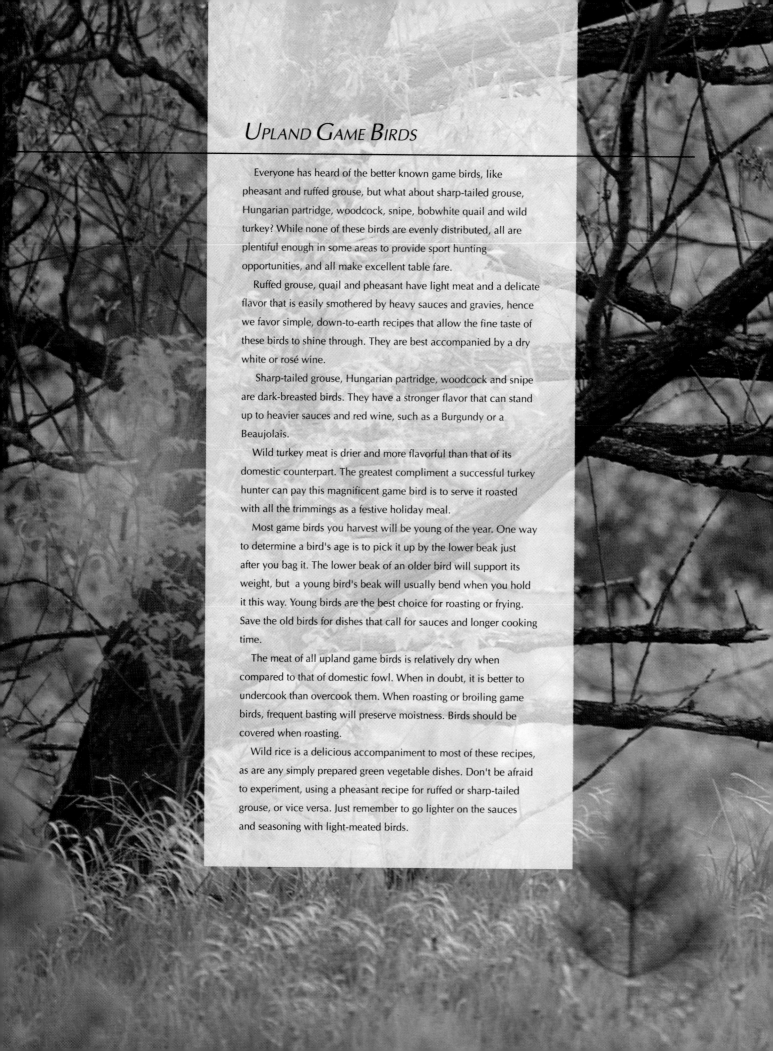

Upland Game Birds

Everyone has heard of the better known game birds, like pheasant and ruffed grouse, but what about sharp-tailed grouse, Hungarian partridge, woodcock, snipe, bobwhite quail and wild turkey? While none of these birds are evenly distributed, all are plentiful enough in some areas to provide sport hunting opportunities, and all make excellent table fare.

Ruffed grouse, quail and pheasant have light meat and a delicate flavor that is easily smothered by heavy sauces and gravies, hence we favor simple, down-to-earth recipes that allow the fine taste of these birds to shine through. They are best accompanied by a dry white or rosé wine.

Sharp-tailed grouse, Hungarian partridge, woodcock and snipe are dark-breasted birds. They have a stronger flavor that can stand up to heavier sauces and red wine, such as a Burgundy or a Beaujolais.

Wild turkey meat is drier and more flavorful than that of its domestic counterpart. The greatest compliment a successful turkey hunter can pay this magnificent game bird is to serve it roasted with all the trimmings as a festive holiday meal.

Most game birds you harvest will be young of the year. One way to determine a bird's age is to pick it up by the lower beak just after you bag it. The lower beak of an older bird will support its weight, but a young bird's beak will usually bend when you hold it this way. Young birds are the best choice for roasting or frying. Save the old birds for dishes that call for sauces and longer cooking time.

The meat of all upland game birds is relatively dry when compared to that of domestic fowl. When in doubt, it is better to undercook than overcook them. When roasting or broiling game birds, frequent basting will preserve moistness. Birds should be covered when roasting.

Wild rice is a delicious accompaniment to most of these recipes, as are any simply prepared green vegetable dishes. Don't be afraid to experiment, using a pheasant recipe for ruffed or sharp-tailed grouse, or vice versa. Just remember to go lighter on the sauces and seasoning with light-meated birds.

BRAISED WILD TURKEY

1 wild turkey

salt and pepper

1 pound salt pork, sliced

1 bay leaf

1/8 teaspoon thyme

1 onion, sliced

1 carrot, sliced

1 large stalk celery, chopped

3 sprigs fresh parsley

1 quart bouillon

Wash turkey with cold running water and pat dry with paper towels. Sprinkle cavity with salt and pepper to taste. Place half of the salt pork inside the turkey and arrange the rest to cover it. Secure with toothpicks if necessary. Roast at 400° for 1 hour. Discard salt pork. Combine remaining ingredients and pour over turkey. Cover tightly and roast for 2 to 3 hours at 300° or until tender, basting frequently.
  6 to 8 servings

ROAST WILD TURKEY

1 10 to 12 pound wild turkey

salt and pepper

Stuffing Ingredients:

1 onion, chopped

1 pound pork sausage

6 cups soft bread crumbs

2 teaspoons salt

1/4 teaspoon pepper

3 tablespoons parsley, chopped

4 slices bacon

Wash turkey under cold running water and pat dry with paper towels. Sprinkle turkey inside and out with salt and pepper to taste. Cook onion and sausage over medium heat in a heavy skillet for 5 minutes or until onion is tender. Combine bread crumbs, salt and pepper in a large bowl. Add onion and sausage; mix well. Mix in a little hot water if stuffing mixture is too dry. Lightly stuff and close both cavities of the turkey and place breast-side down in a roasting pan. Roast uncovered at 325° for 10 minutes per pound of turkey (weight before stuffing). Turn turkey breast-side up and place bacon slices on breast. Continue cooking uncovered for 10 to 12 minutes more per pound. Turkey is done when juices run clear when a fork is pushed into the thickest part of the thigh.
  6 to 8 servings

Turkey hunting, unlike hunting for other game species, is a springtime sport. When oak leaves first appear, meadows begin to green up and morning fog hangs heavy in every valley, the turkey hunter blends into the landscape and yelps, clucks and purrs like a lovesick hen to attract a gobbler.

The first thing you notice, sitting silently with your back against an oak, is that the spring woods are alive with sound. On a November deer stand, you may hear a woodpecker rapping on a dead limb, or a pair of squirrels racing up and down a trunk, but most other creatures are silent or absent. In April, though, it seems that every woodland resident has a song to share with the world.

Barred owls signal an end to their nightly vigil with a haunting "who-who who-whoo-ah", as the first gray fingers of light spread across the eastern sky. Soon after, thrushes and other songbirds greet the dawn with an outpouring of trills, warbles and melodies from every hollow, every bush, every possible vantage point as the the day begins. Ruffed grouse, tireless drummers this time of year, beat out their rolling "thump, thump, thump, ump-ump-ump-ump-p-p-p-p-p-p-p" sometimes all night long and well into the morning.

And above this joyous din rises the thunderous "gobble-obble-obble-obble" of a boss gobbler telling all who would hear that he is still king of the mountain.

When a gobbler flies down from his roost, there is no telling how soon he will come to your calling. He might come in a matter of minutes, or he might take an hour or more. He might come strutting and shaking the ground with his booming gobbles, or he might sneak in unannounced. And he might not come at all, leaving you to ponder your choice of calls, your position and the wonderful uncertainty of this hunt where you play the siren to a heedless sailor. (Dan)

PHEASANT WITH RICE DRESSING

1 plucked pheasant

1/2 cup long grain rice

1/3 cup wild rice

3/4 teaspoon onion powder

1-1/2 tablespoons parsley flakes

2 tablespoons finely ground celery

3/4 teaspoon garlic powder

1/2 teaspoon sugar

1/4 teaspoon salt

1/4 teaspoon pepper

chicken bouillon

1/2 pound mushrooms

3 tablespoons butter, divided

1 cup dairy sour cream

Make 1-1/2 cups of bouillon at one-half recommended strength and add spices, 1 tablespoon butter, and ground celery. Bring to a boil and add long grain rice. Cook until bouillon is absorbed. Cook wild rice according to directions. Sauté sliced mushrooms in butter. Mix long grain rice, wild rice and mushrooms together. Fill body cavity of bird and place remaining dressing in covered baking dish. Bake pheasant 1-1/2 hours at 350°. Bake covered rice dish for 20 minutes, or until heated through.

Sauce for pheasant and rice:

reserved drippings from pheasant

dairy sour cream (approximately 1/2 cup)

salt and pepper

Drain pheasant drippings into saucepan. Add sour cream slowly to desired richness or thickness. Salt and pepper to taste. Heat on low before serving.

2 servings

The ring-necked pheasant is an exotic species, brought to this continent from China and introduced in Oregon's Willamette Valley in the 1880s. Through repeated stocking and natural reproduction, pheasants have made themselves at home in suitable habitat from coast to coast.

Modern farming practices, especially fence-to-fence planting and early mowing of alfalfa, have drastically reduced populations of wild pheasants in many areas over the past several decades. Today, pheasant hunting is sustained across much of the Midwest thanks in part to stocking programs run by state wildlife agencies and local sportsmen's clubs. (Dan)

SWEET AND SOUR PHEASANT

1 pheasant, boned and cut into cubes

2 tablespoons vegetable oil

1 16-ounce can chunk pineapple

3 tablespoons cornstarch

1/4 cup brown sugar

1/4 cup white vinegar

5 to 6 tablespoons soy sauce

1/4 cup chopped green pepper

3 tablespoons chopped onion

Brown pheasant in oil. Cover with about one cup of water and simmer for 1 hour or until tender. Drain off liquid. Drain pineapple, reserving the juice. Mix pineapple juice, cornstarch, vinegar, brown sugar and soy sauce. Add to meat and cook over medium heat until mixture becomes thick. Add peppers, onion and pineapple. Heat thoroughly. Serve over rice.

3 to 4 servings

PHEASANT KIEV

boned breasts of 2 pheasants

1/4 pound butter, softened

1 teaspoon finely chopped parsley

1 small garlic clove, finely chopped

a shake of cayenne pepper

3/4 cup flour

1 egg, beaten

1-1/2 cups dry bread crumbs

vegetable oil for deep fat frying

With a mallet fatten each breast between waxed paper to 1/2 inch thickness. Place thin filets in the refrigerator for 2 hours.

Mix the parsley, garlic and cayenne with the softened butter and shape the butter into four egg-shaped balls. Place the butter in the freezer until the pheasant is chilled.

After 2 hours, brush one side of each pheasant filet with beaten egg. Place a piece of butter on the egg-coated side of each filet and fold the meat over to make an envelope. Secure the edges with toothpicks. Roll each filet in flour, dip into beaten egg, and then roll it in bread crumbs.

Heat oil to 375° in a deep-fat fryer. Carefully place the filets in a frying basket and lower into fat. Cook 7 to 8 minutes or until golden brown. Serve immediately.

3 to 4 servings

Serve with rice pilaf and a side dish of steamed asparagus.

CURRIED PHEASANT

1 pheasant, cut into serving pieces

1 tablespoon butter

1 cup chopped pared apple

1/2 cup chopped onion

1 cup sliced celery

1 clove garlic, finely chopped

3 tablespoons curry powder

3/4 teaspoon salt

3/4 cup chicken broth

1 4-ounce can sliced mushrooms, drained

2 cups milk

2 tablespoons cornstarch

Condiments: Shredded coconut, chopped peanuts, raisins

Preheat oven to 325°. Arrange pheasant pieces on cookie sheet. Bake for 20 minutes to par-cook. While pheasant is in the oven, melt butter in large skillet. Add apple, onion, celery and garlic. Sauté until onion is soft. Combine curry powder, salt, chicken broth, mushrooms and milk in a mixing bowl and stir into skillet mixture. Add pheasant pieces, cover and cook for 20 minutes, or until pheasant is tender, occasionally spooning sauce over pheasant.

Remove pheasant pieces to a platter of hot rice. Stir cornstarch into small amount of cold water until smooth; then slowly stir into skillet mixture. Cook and stir until mixture thickens and bubbles. Pour over pheasant pieces and serve. Pass shredded coconut, chopped peanuts and raisins.

2 to 3 servings

Given a choice, a pheasant will usually run rather than fly. Hunting them without a dog is a great way to get plenty of exercise, but don't count on seeing many birds! A well-trained dog increases your odds of seeing and getting shots at pheasants, and most bird dogs will track downed game adequately enough to ensure that few cripples are lost.

Serious pheasant hunters will forever debate the merits of one breed of dog over another. I'm biased toward springers, but that's because I've owned and hunted over them for many years. I've also enjoyed many a hunt over Brittanies, Labs and Golden Retrievers. The bottom line is simple: a pheasant dog must have the stamina to bust through cattails and canary grass all day, the nose to trail a runner or a cripple, and the desire to stay with this crazy game as long as you do. (Dan)

PHEASANT DIVIN

2 cups or more cubed cooked pheasant
  (bake in pan 35 minutes at 350°)

2 10-ounce packages frozen broccoli spears
  (cook 5 minutes and drain)

2 10-1/2 ounce cans cream of chicken soup

1/2 cup mayonnaise

1/2 cup sour cream

1 teaspoon lemon juice

1/2 teaspoon curry powder (can be omitted)

1/2 cup bread crumbs browned in 2 tablespoons butter

1/2 cup grated sharp cheddar cheese

Arrange broccoli in shallow casserole. Place pheasant over broccoli. Combine soup, mayonnaise, sour cream, lemon juice (and curry powder, see above); and heat mixture. Pour over ingredients in casserole. Sprinkle with grated cheese and buttered bread crumbs.

Bake at 350° for 25 to 30 minutes (glass pan, at 325°). Note: If made ahead of time and refrigerated, bake at above temperatures for about 45 minutes.

6 servings

SKINNY'S LIGHT PHEASANT AND RICE

4 pheasant breast halves

1/3 cup bottled Italian salad dressing

1-1/2 cups cooked rice

1 bag (16 ounces) frozen broccoli, carrots, water chestnuts
  and red pepper combination

1 can (2.8 ounces) French-fried onions

1 cup bouillon

3/4 teaspoon Italian seasoning

Place pheasant breasts in 8 x 12 inch baking dish. Pour salad dressing over pheasant. Bake, uncovered, at 350° for 15 minutes. Place rice, 1/2 can onions, and thawed vegetables around and under pheasant.

Combine bouillon and Italian seasoning; pour over pheasant. Bake uncovered at 350° for 25 minutes. Top with remaining onions and bake 2 to 3 minutes longer. Let stand 5 minutes before serving.

3 to 4 servings

SOUR CREAM PHEASANTS

2 pheasants, cut into serving-sized pieces

1-1/2 cups flour

salt and pepper

3 tablespoons butter

3 tablespoons cooking oil

1 cup dairy sour cream

2 cups water (more if needed)

2 teaspoons celery salt

1 teaspoon garlic salt

Dredge pheasant pieces in flour seasoned with salt and pepper. Brown pieces in butter and oil. Discard excess oil. Arrange pieces in baking pan. In separate dish, mix sour cream, water, celery salt and garlic salt. Pour over pheasants and bake at 350° for 2 hours or until tender. Baste occasionally with gravy to keep pheasant moist.
4 to 6 servings
Serve with a baked potato.

PHEASANT IN MUSHROOM GRAVY

1 pheasant, boned

1 10-3/4 ounce can cream of mushroom soup

1 tablespoon soy sauce

seasoned salt, to taste

paprika

Place pheasant in baking dish. Mix soup, soy sauce and seasoned salt in measuring cup. Add enough water to make 2 cups. Stir. Pour over pheasant. Sprinkle with paprika. Bake uncovered at 375° for 1 to 1-1/2 hours or until tender. Baste occasionally with gravy. Serve with rice or potatoes.
2 to 3 servings

GOURMET QUAIL

8 quail
salt and pepper
1/2 cup extra virgin olive oil
1 carrot, chopped
1/2 pound fresh peas, shelled
1 zucchini, chopped

6 mushrooms, chopped
2 shallots, minced
4 tablespoons butter
1/2 cup dry red wine
1 cup chicken stock
2 slices foie gras

Salt and pepper quail inside and out and truss. Lightly sauté in oil in a large skillet until golden brown on all sides. Remove and keep warm. Add carrots and peas and cook for 5 to 10 minutes. Add zucchini and mushrooms, cook 5 minutes more. Sauté shallots in butter in a large pan. Add wine and stock and reduce it to 1 cup. Add vegetables and quail and simmer, uncovered, for 10 minutes. Stir in the foie gras and mix well.
4 servings
Serve over wild rice with a tossed salad.

SAUTEED QUAIL IN GRAPE SAUCE

6 quail
2 teaspoons salt
1/4 teaspoon white pepper
1 teaspoon shortening
1 tablespoon butter
1 teaspoon tarragon leaves
1 tablespoon shallots, finely chopped
1/2 cup white wine
1/2 cup chicken stock
1/4 cup light cream
2 tablespoons cornstarch
1 egg yolk, beaten
1-1/2 cups seedless grapes

Salt and pepper quail to taste; brown lightly on all sides in shortening and butter in a Dutch oven or other heavy pot. Combine tarragon, shallots, wine and stock; pour over quail. Simmer for 20 minutes or until tender, basting occasionally. Remove quail and keep warm. Blend cream, cornstarch, egg yolk and add to sauce, stirring constantly until thickened. Return quail to the sauce, add grapes and heat thoroughly.
3 servings
Serve with steamed corn.

BAKED GROUSE IN WINE

1 plucked grouse per person
1-1/2 cups poultry stuffing per bird
1/4 cup dry white wine per bird
melted butter
poultry seasoning

Stuff birds and brush them generously with melted butter. Place birds breast up on heavy-duty aluminum foil and pour wine over birds. Sprinkle breasts with seasoning and seal foil. Place wrapped birds in shallow roasting pan and bake for 45 minutes at 425°. Open foil and turn heat down to 350° and allow bird to brown for 15 minutes, watching carefully. Remove birds from foil and place on a bed of wild rice. Pour wine drippings over rice and serve.

Aldo Leopold is widely recognized as the father of modern wildlife management, but few people know he was also a grouse hunting fanatic. In A SAND COUNTY ALMANAC, he wrote: "There are two kinds of hunting: ordinary hunting, and ruffed grouse hunting."

For Leopold, and for others who are drawn to the aspen woods, alder runs and raspberry thickets each October, the goal of these outings is the pulse-quickening flush of a grouse that always startles, no matter how many times they have heard it. The beginning hunter often finds grouse frustrating, since they frequent dense cover and rarely offer a clear shot. Every grouse hunter I know carries a clear picture in his mind of the first ruff he ever shot in flight.

For my taste, Leopold might well have added: "And there are two kinds of eating: ordinary eating, and eating ruffed grouse." I think if I could choose my last meal, it would be baked grouse, accompanied by wild rice, homemade wild cranberry sauce and a delicate white wine. And for dessert, without hesitation I'd opt for wild raspberry shortcake. See you in heaven! (Dan)

SLOW-COOKED GROUSE SOUP

1 grouse, cut into pieces and boned, or equivalent

5 carrots, cut into pieces

2 medium onions, quartered

2 stalks celery, coarsely chopped

2 or 3 leeks

2 bay leaves

salt and pepper

Place all ingredients in slow cooker and fill with water to within an inch of the top. Add salt and pepper to taste. Cover and set cooker on high. Allow soup to simmer for 8 hours or so. Add salt to taste if necessary. Turn heat down to low until ready to serve. Timing is not critical for this recipe, you can let it go another hour or two with no harm done. If you will be away for 12 hours or more, use the low or medium setting throughout cooking time. Leftover soup may be frozen in plastic containers.

Always be sure to remove and discard bay leaves before serving!

Grouse soup prepared in a slow-cooker has at least three things going for it. First, it literally cooks by itself: you can start it the night before, and in the morning have a hearty soup to pack in a wide-mouth thermos for lunch, or start it in the morning and supper will be ready when you come home from work or an outing. Second, it is a great way to make use of the occasional bird you center at close range, leftovers and/or carcasses that remain from other recipes. And third, it is absolutely delicious. After tasting this soup, you will never again settle for chicken noodle! (Nancy)

Most grouse hunting partners personalize their favorite coverts by giving them names that refer obscurely to the owner of the property or commemorate some noteworthy event the partners shared there. That way, they can talk about "Widow's Orchard," "Tom's Double" or "Last Chance Pasture" without revealing their whereabouts to would-be interlopers.

Steve Duren and I used to hunt a covert that for years we simply named after the dirt road that dead-ended there. The covert was an 80-acre aspen woods that had been logged a year or two before we started hunting it. Centuries of spring runoff had cut deeply into the clay soil, creating several steep ravines that we liked to walk for grouse. Each year the grouse hunting there got better as young aspen saplings grew up thick as the hair on a dog to provide good cover for the birds and other wildlife.

On one late fall hunt, Steve and I were working up one of these ravines, he on one shoulder and I on the other, when he suddenly stopped, grabbed the dog, then backed up and crossed the ravine toward me. He was pale as he hustled, wide-eyed, up the slope.

"I almost stepped on a bear," he panted.

"You're kidding!" I replied.

"It was either a bear or a black angus," he said, pointing across the ravine. "It was all curled up just the other side of that deadfall."

Steve held the dog while I sneaked back along the route he had taken for a look at this thing. All I found was what looked like a giant bird nest made of leaves, snug up against the log he had pointed to. Apparently he had surprised a bear that had chosen that deadfall for its winter den, and it had slipped away without a sound while he was retreating.

We never saw that bruin again, not that day nor any other, but from that moment on we called that covert "Sleeping Bear." (Dan)

LEMON BROILED GROUSE

2 grouse breasts

salt

1 teaspoon thyme

3 tablespoons butter, divided

3 tablespoons lemon juice, divided

Lightly salt breasts and place in microwave on high for 1-1/2 minutes. Turn and continue cooking for 1 minute more. Cool until able to handle, then butter breasts and rub with thyme. Place on broiling pan and drizzle with 2 tablespoons lemon juice. Broil for 5 minutes or until done. Serve with mixed melted butter and lemon juice.

2 servings

Serve with buttered sweet potatoes and a green salad with a light white wine.

WILD RICE DRESSING

2 cups wild rice (washed several times, soaked in hot water
   2 hours and drained)

3 quarts hot water

1 stick butter

1/2 cup chopped green pepper

1 cup chopped onion

1 cup chopped celery

1/2 pound fried, crumbled bacon

1 cup canned chicken broth

Boil water and add wild rice. Cover, and continue boiling for 5 minutes. Turn off heat and let stand for 1/2 hour. Drain off excess water, if any. Melt butter in frying pan and add green pepper, onion and celery. Cook slowly until tender. Add vegetables, chicken broth and bacon to wild rice. Stir until well mixed; place in baking dish and bake at 325° for 40 minutes.

Sauce for wild rice:

2 cans (10-1/2 ounces) cream of mushroom soup

1 can (8 ounces) sliced mushrooms with juice

Heat ingredients and serve in separate bowl.

HUNGARIAN PARTRIDGE WITH RICE STUFFING

4 Hungarian partridge, whole

1 tablespoon salt

1-1/2 cups long grain rice

1/2 cup butter or margarine

1 cup celery, finely chopped

3 tablespoons minced onion

1/2 cup fresh mushrooms,
   sliced, or canned and drained

1/8 teaspoon sage

1/8 teaspoon thyme

1/8 teaspoon savory

melted butter or margarine

6 slices bacon

Sprinkle the cavity of each bird with one teaspoon salt. Brown rice in a dry skillet. Place rice in large saucepan , add 3 cups water and 1 teaspoon salt, cook until done. Sauté celery, onions and mushrooms in butter for 10 minutes. Mix vegetables and herbs with rice. Stuff the birds lightly and tie or skewer closed. Cover breasts with bacon. Place in a Dutch oven or covered baking dish and bake at 350° for about 2 hours or until tender, basting frequently. Any extra stuffing can be baked in a covered dish during the last 30 minutes of the roasting time.

6 to 8 servings

Serve with steamed asparagus spears and a sliced tomato salad with vinaigrette dressing.

Waterfowl

Liberal bag limits and endless flights of migrating ducks that darken the skies are a thing of the past. The modern duck hunter has learned to savor the smell of an October marsh and the beauty of a hazy sunrise or an approaching squall slanting toward him across open water. He is content to call a bag of two or three ducks a good day's hunt. And perhaps that same hunter appreciates the meal or two those few ducks will provide far more today than he might have in an earlier time when wild duck was regular fare.

Hunters still enjoy fair shooting at mallards and teal, and the comeback of the flashy wood duck is testimony to the hard work of many dedicated conservationists. There may be fewer ducks today, but it's hard to find a place in the northern states in the fall where the raucous cries of Canada geese aren't heard and where their ragged V's aren't etched across the evening sky.

The taste of waterfowl varies with the species and age of the bird, and — most importantly — what the bird has been eating. A duck that has subsisted on a diet of fish will smell like it and require marinating in something potent or stuffing with quartered apple, orange or potato (to be discarded before the bird is served) to make it palatable.

A duck that is plump and whose skin is pale and flesh light in color will be more tender and taste better than a scrawny, dark-meated, orange-skinned bird. Younger ducks and geese are best for roasting. You can usually tell a duck's relative age by twisting the leg and wing joints. Birds hatched this year will have softer joints that come apart easily. Most older birds' joints resist twisting. Save them for braising or stewing.

The true wild duck gourmet prefers his birds cooked rare in an extremely hot oven. Waterfowl should be cooked covered, with the skin left on, and basted liberally. A dried-out, overcooked duck might make a good football, but you wouldn't want to eat it.

SIMPLY DUCK

1 plucked mallard or other large duck

1 onion

1 apple

small bunch of celery

a handful of grapes

6 strips of bacon (optional)

orange juice (optional)

melted butter (optional)

red wine (optional)

Quarter onion. Rub cut side of onion on cleaned and dried skin of the duck. Salt and pepper the duck and put onion, along with cubed apple, short celery stalks and grapes, in the cavity of the duck.

Optional: Tack bacon strips to breasts of ducks with toothpicks before roasting.

Place ducks on rack in a covered roasting pan and roast at 325° for 2 hours, or until tender.

Optional: If ducks need basting, use orange juice, melted butter, or melted butter and red wine rather than pan drippings.

Remove vegetables from the cavity of the bird and discard. Remove bacon and discard. Serve simply.

2 servings

Serve with cauliflower au gratin and spinach salad.

Hunting ducks over decoys is a weather-dependent sport: the nastier the weather, the better the shooting. It's not that ducks like the kind of windy, rainy day that folks say is a "nice day if you're a duck." It's just that they fly in that kind of weather, which makes them suckers for a spread of decoys tucked into a cozy-looking pothole out of the wind in the corner of a marsh.

On calm, sunny days, ducks loll around just like people, in no hurry to go anywhere because they're quite comfortable right where they are. On such days, the ducks are always off in some other part of the marsh. You can hear them quacking and chuckling to themselves, but you'll spend a quiet, lonely morning in your blind.

That's exactly what happened the day we taped our first duck hunting segment. The evening before, Hack Noyes and I had camouflaged our blind and carefully cut out a spot nearby in the cattails where we would hide our camera crew in their boat. Peter Van Housen and our crew—cinematographer Marshall Savick and engineer Airel Mitcham—met us early the next morning, and before daylight we were all in place, waiting for something to happen.

What happened was this: the sun came up in a gorgeous azure sky, but nary a duck showed itself. There was not a breeze to ripple the water, so Marshall shot some stunning footage of autumn foliage on the far bank mirrored in the lake's surface. A lone Canada goose spiraled down a couple hundred yards from us, then swam toward our decoys through the mist, honking quizzically and pushing a gentle wave ahead of it as it came. Goose season was closed, so we let it be.

Marshall taped the goose's arrival as well as the passage of a pair of whitetails on the far bank. Just for fun, Peter set out a couple antique decoys, mallards with the sloping bill and milk-bottle shape that identifies them as Masons—highly prized by collectors. When we picked up and left at mid-morning, Hack and I kidded Peter, blaming him and his Masons for our lack of success, but we all knew the truth: it was just too nice a day. (Dan)

OVEN BARBECUED DUCK

2 ducks, halved

1/4 cup melted butter

1/4 cup lemon juice

1 clove garlic, minced

1/4 cup salad oil

1 tablespoon onion, grated

1 tablespoon paprika

1/2 cup catsup

1/4 teaspoon pepper

Place duck halves, skin side up, in a shallow baking pan. Rub with garlic and brush with melted butter. Roast for 10 minutes at 400°.

Combine other ingredients in a small saucepan and heat to a simmer. Reduce oven temperature to 350° and baste with sauce every 10 minutes until ducks are done.

4 servings

Serve with steak fries and buttered corn.

Opening day is sacred to a waterfowler. Most duck hunters spend the first day of the season on their favorite marsh, arriving well before the noon shooting hour to put a few more reeds around the blind, set out the blocks, eat lunch and just see what local birds are around this year. While I do enjoy shooting over decoys, there's something about floating a river in October that makes me choose jump shooting, hands down, as my first duck hunt of the year.

When I was teaching, my calendar read "waterfowl meeting" on October 1st, and I always managed to cancel afternoon classes or weasel out of faculty meetings so I could meet Steve Duren at the river for our ritual first hunt of the year. More often than not, our opening day float took place under a warm, Indian summer sun.

Big trout, up from downriver on their spawning run, bulged the surface as they fed. We always said next year we'd come here with our fly rods a week before duck season, when trout season was still open, but we never got around to it.

We always saw ducks on those float trips and usually shot a mallard or two, and maybe a woodie or blue-wing. On a rare occasion we'd down a grouse that flushed from the river bank.

The main attraction of those trips, though, was the sensory feast of a world not yet ready for winter: The burgundy stems of bankside red osiers that shone through a pale screen of rose and amber; the tag alders still in cool, verdant leaf whose shade hid those brightest of gems — the wood ducks — until they burst, squealing, from cover, sending shards of sun and water in all directions; the pungent brew of a hundred smells as the woods and swamp digested another summer's richness; and always the pull, the irresistible pull of the river. (Dan)

Mint Duck with Vegetables

2 mallard-sized ducks, plucked

1/2 cup butter

1-1/2 tablespoons dried mint, reconstituted in hot water

4 potatoes, peeled and quartered

4 large turnips, peeled and halved

4 carrots, peeled and cut into 2-inch chunks

2 tablespoons cooking oil

1/8 teaspoon cayenne

salt and pepper

Whip the butter; add mint and season to taste with salt, pepper and cayenne. Whip again. Carefully pull the skin away from the breast of the duck and butter the meat over as large an area as possible. Sauté potatoes, turnips and carrots in cooking oil. Arrange vegetables around ducks in a roasting pan and cook for 15 minutes at 400°. Reduce heat to 325° and cook for another 30 minutes or until done.

4 servings

This dish is a meal in itself and might be followed by a fruit dessert or pineapple upside-down cake.

Citrus Grilled Duck

4 small ducks, such as wood duck, teal or bufflehead

4 lemons, thinly sliced

1 sweet red onion, peeled and sliced

salt and pepper

1 teaspoon oregano

olive oil

Place onion slices in a layer in a roasting pan. Butterfly each duck by first cutting along both sides of the backbone and removing it. Bend the legs forward, joints out, and insert the tips into two slits cut just below the breast meat. Bend the wings down over the breast. Press down on the entire bird to flatten. Season with salt, pepper and oregano. Place breast-side up on top of the onions. Cover completely with lemon slices and brush with olive oil. Cover and refrigerate overnight.

Remove and set aside lemon slices. Brush ducks with olive oil. Grill quickly on both sides, bone side first. Return to roasting pan, replace the lemon slices and brush with olive oil. Roast for 30 to 40 minutes, or until done, at 350°. Season to taste with salt and pepper.

Variation: Substitute oranges or limes for lemons.

4 servings

A vegetable side dish choice might be steamed sliced zucchini and onions.

Stuffed Goose With Plum Sauce

1 large goose

salt and pepper

1 lemon

4 slices bacon

Chestnut Dressing Ingredients:

1/2 cup butter

goose giblets, chopped

1 cup chopped onions

1cup chopped celery

1 clove garlic, minced

1/2 cup chopped parsley

2 cups cooked wild rice

3 cups chestnuts, boiled and chopped

2 cups apples, peeled, cored and chopped

1/2 cup raisins

3/4 cup Cassis or other black-currant liqueur, divided

1 cup brandy or white wine

1 teaspoon poultry seasoning

1 teaspoon cinnamon

Plum Sauce Ingredients:

1 cup port wine

1/3 cup goose drippings

1 30-ounce can pitted purple plums, drained

1/2 teaspoon cinnamon

1/8 teaspoon cayenne

1 tablespoon cornstarch

Soak raisins in 1/2 cup of the Cassis. Sauté giblets, onions, celery, garlic and parsley in butter in a deep skillet. Add rice and chestnuts. Mix well. Add apples, raisins, brandy or wine, poultry seasoning, cinnamon and an additional 2 tablespoons Cassis. Mix again. Rub the goose inside and out with lemon juice seasoned to taste with salt and pepper. Fill both cavities of the bird loosely with stuffing and skewer or tie closed. Any extra stuffing can be baked in a covered casserole during the goose's last 45 minutes cooking time. Fold the wings under the body and tie; tie the legs together. Place breast-side up in a roasting pan. Place bacon slices on the breast to keep it from drying out. Roast, uncovered, for 2-1/2 hours at 325° basting frequently with pan drippings. Sprinkle remaining Cassis on goose and continue cooking for an additional 10 minutes.

To make the plum sauce: Slowly heat the wine for 2 or 3 minutes in a medium saucepan. Add the pan drippings and cook for another 3 minutes. Break the plums up a bit with a fork and add to the wine. Add cinnamon and cayenne. Simmer for 5 minutes. Combine cornstarch with 2 tablespoons water to make a smooth paste; add to the sauce. Bring to a boil, stirring constantly. Simmer for about 20 minutes, stirring occasionally, until the sauce is thickened and translucent.

4 to 6 servings

GOOSE AU FEU

1 goose

2 tablespoons salt

2 pounds lean beef or venison, cut into cubes

1 pound beef or venison bones, cracked

1 pound carrots

1 pound turnips

1 pound leeks

1 clove garlic, minced

1/2 teaspoon pepper

1 bay leaf

1/8 teaspoon thyme

1 cup white wine

Remove skin from goose, wash , dry with paper towels and split in half. Dissolve salt in 4 quarts of water in a large Dutch oven or other pot with a lid. Add goose halves, beef or venison and bones. Add enough water to cover, adding additional salt if necessary. Bring slowly to boil, skimming off the scum frequently. Add vegetables cut into chunks, garlic, pepper, bay leaf, thyme and wine. Discard all bone. Serve the vegetables over dry French bread, with stock poured over all. Carve the goose and serve with the red meat.

8 servings

During our first season we learned a lot about the making of television. One thing we knew, though, was that everything has to look just right, particularly under the hot studio lights.

For our first Christmas show, Dan and I cooked a Canada goose. The bird we had to work with was young and tender, but loaded with pinfeathers. When Dan finished plucking it the night before the taping session, dozens of dark, ugly pinfeathers remained imbedded in the breast skin. We knew that although they would not harm the flavor of the bird, they would look terrible under the studio kitchen lights, so we had to get them out at all costs.

It was no use to singe the bird, since all that remained were the pulpy feather bases, so we tried tweezers but could not get those stubborn pinfeathers out. It was late and we were desperate, so we tried a disposable razor. To our relief it worked!

Those pinfeathers came off, along with the outer layer of skin, leaving the bird with a clean, smooth breast that looked great on camera. We're willing to bet that's the first time a goose was ever shaved for a TV appearance. (Nancy)

GOOSE BREAST SAUTERNE

1 boneless goose breast per serving
1/2 cup sauterne
1/2 teaspoon salt
1/4 teaspoon pepper
1/2 teaspoon garlic salt
1/2 cup flour
vegetable oil

Multiply all seasoning ingredients by the number of breasts being pre-pared. Cut the breasts in half and pound with a meat hammer to ten-derize. Mix salt, pepper, garlic salt and flour in a bag. Shake with breasts to coat. Brown goose breasts very slowly in oil in a heavy skillet. Mix sauterne with an equal amount of water and pour over meat. Simmer until tender. Serve with wild rice.

I have never shot a goose on camera. Early in our first season, director Jack Abrams and I took our camera crew to Monroe County, where Tom Muench had invited us to hunt geese with him. We sat in a cornfield all morning in the rain while geese flew overhead out of range. When the segment aired, I got a dozen offers of "guaranteed" goose hunts. Next season I hunt-ed with woodcarver Tom Strauss near Fond du Lac, in the Horicon Zone. Tom always saves his Horicon permit for the last day and then goes out in the afternoon. "To make it more sport-ing," he says.

Tom had never failed to shoot his Horicon goose until the year we joined him, when both he and I failed to fill our tags.

The next season, I joined Wisconsin Waterfowlers Association founder Jerry Solsrud, again in the Horicon Zone. We came closer this time — Jerry called in a goose, but my shot missed the mark.

Encouraged, I asked Jerry to give me another chance the next year when I drew two tags for the December Horicon Zone hunt. Five hunters, along with cinematographer Marshall Savick and engineer Ken Kobylarz, stood on a wooded hilltop overlooking a lake where an estimated 40,000 geese honked up a din that would put the L.A. Freeway to shame.

We waited for three hours, while small groups left the gigantic gaggle and flew out to raid the surrounding grainfields. They flew in every direction, except over our heads.

Finally, Bill Maund and Jim Shurtz slipped off to get under the flight path most of the geese were taking. Bill came back with his two geese, so we made him the hero.

Half an hour later, Doug Linn filled his tags; then a pair of Canadas finally came over within range, and I doubled. You'll never see me make that shot on television, though, because we had already sent Kenny and Marshall home, preserving intact my perfect 0-for-4 on-camera goose hunt record. (Dan)

Venison

While the term venison has long been used as a generic word for wild meat of any kind, it usually refers to such big game as deer, elk and moose. The recipes in this chapter will yield tasty results with similar cuts of most big game animals, but they were designed for preparing the "venison" best known to Midwestern hunters — the white-tailed deer.

Venison is the staple wild game of most hunters, and the annual gun deer hunt is an important tradition, celebrated in many hunting families with as much ceremony and enthusiasm as the Fourth of July or Christmas. With modern game management practices helping to maintain large and healthy deer herds, the annual hunt in most deer camps produces enough venison to give all hunters a taste of fall.

Generally the meat of a young doe will be more tender and tastier than that of an older buck taken during or after the rut, and farmland deer that have fed on alfalfa and corn will often produce sweeter venison than deer from the north woods. Cared for properly, venison from any healthy deer will delight the palate.

Venison is leaner and more flavorful, but — if properly aged — as tender as any prime beef. You won't find venison steaks and roasts marbled with fat. On a deer, the fat — or tallow — lies outside the muscle tissue and between layers of muscle. Venison tallow should always be trimmed off before cooking or freezing because it imparts a strong taste to the meat and may turn rancid if left on meat that is frozen for long periods.

Venison steaks, chops and roasts are at their juicy best when served rare. Venison can dry out, lose its flavor and become tough and stringy if overcooked. Slow cooking in a covered pan at lower temperatures than used for beef works best for venison roasts. Steaks and chops should be cut at least an inch thick. If you grill or oven broil them, baste them frequently with butter and broil them for only a minute or two on a side.

Venison, like all game, should always be served piping hot on a heated platter. Wait until your guests are seated before you bring your venison roast or steaks to the table, and be sure to allow enough for seconds because venison lovers have a habit of coming back for more.

VENISON ITALIAN NOODLES

1 pound ground venison

1 cup elbow macaroni noodles

1 8-ounce can tomato sauce

1 6-ounce can tomato paste

2 teaspoons Italian spices

3/4 teaspoon garlic powder

2 to 2-1/2 ounces mozzarella cheese

2 to 2-1/2 ounces colby cheese

dab of butter

Brown the venison gently in a small amount of butter in a small saucepan. Cook the elbow noodles according to package directions. Combine tomato sauce, paste, spices and garlic in a saucepan and heat to a slow boil. With buttered cooked noodles in a bowl, combine the tomato sauce with the venison and pour over the noodles. Add cheese and stir until cheese is melted.

Noodle dish may be served immediately or put in a casserole dish, covered with additional cheese (perhaps Parmesan), and baked at 350° until the top is golden brown.

3 to 4 servings

A plain green vegetable like brocolli goes well with this noodle dish.

A lot of my recipes don't start out as recipes at all. I like to play with different flavor combinations. If an improvised recipe works, I might write it down for future use. If it doesn't, I chalk it up to the fun of experimentation.

I often end up with little time to prepare an elaborate meal. When that happens, I toss a pound of ground venison (we like ours straight — not cut with pork or beef suet) in the microwave to thaw and check to see what else is in the larder. Even when I am "out of everything," there always seem to be enough basics to throw together a reasonable meal.

It's really hard to go wrong with venison, tomato sauce and your favorite cheese and spices. This one worked. (Nancy)

VENISON IN WINE

3 pounds venison, cut in 1-inch cubes
2 bay leaves
1 can cream of mushroom soup
1 can French onion soup
3/4 cup dry red wine
1 8-ounce can sliced mushrooms
1/4 cup brandy

Place all ingredients except brandy in a large casserole. Cover and bake at 350° for 3-1/2 hours. Add brandy and cook 30 minutes longer. Serve over rice, mashed potatoes or egg noodles.
6 servings

MARINATED VENISON KABOBS

1-1/4 pound venison steak, cut into 1-inch cubes
1 to 2 fresh green peppers, cut into chunks
20 whole fresh mushrooms
1 to 2 medium onions, cut into chunks

Marinade ingredients:
1 teaspoon dry mustard
1/4 teaspoon pepper
1/2 cup vegetable oil
1/3 cup soy sauce
1/4 cup red wine vinegar
2 tablespoons lemon juice
1 tablespoon Worchestershire sauce

Combine marinade ingredients. Place venison cubes in marinade, turning to coat completely. Marinate covered for at least 4 hours or overnight, refrigerated. Turn several times. About 30 to 60 minutes before grilling, add the green pepper, mushrooms and onion to the marinade, making sure to coat each piece.
When ready to grill, drain meat and vegetables. Reserve marinade for basting. Alternately thread venison and vegetable pieces onto skewers. Grill kabobs on a greased grill about 3 inches from coals for 10 to 20 minutes or until meat is cooked. Turn often for even browning. Baste frequently.
4 servings
Seasoned white rice or wild rice and a glass of red wine round out this dinner menu.

VENISON HEART IN WINE

1 deer heart
butter
2 to 3 cups beef bouillon
2 to 3 cups red wine

Choose a saucepan which is large enough to brown the deer heart, but also allows you to cover it with liquid. Brown the deer heart in a small amount of butter. Use equal parts of beef bouillion and red wine to cover deer heart in the saucepan. Simmer slowly, covered, until tender (about 2 hours). If desired, thicken juices to make a gravy.

Deer heart is very good served with creamed spinach and a sharp horseradish on the side.

Too many hunters leave the organ meat — heart, liver and kidneys — in the woods because they don't want to fuss with them or don't know what to do with them once they get them home.

There are dozens of recipes for heart. It can be roasted, boiled, baked, served hot or sliced cold for sandwiches. We just learned of a new one we haven't had a chance to try yet — it involves "unrolling" the muscle layers, then laying strips of bacon between them, rolling the heart back up again and roasting it. Sounds delicious! (Nancy)

Most deer hunters hope to tag a buck on opening day, for that's when their chances of doing so are best. Deer numbers are obviously highest before the shooting starts, and the big bucks that have survived several seasons have their minds on does.

I have taken a fair number of bucks on opening day, more, in fact than on all other days combined for all the seasons I've hunted. Still, I have often maintained you don't learn very much by killing a buck on opening morning.

Sure, you know you were in the right place at the right time, but do you know why? How many of us ever bother to backtrack a buck we have just shot to learn where he came from? And, of course, there is no way of knowing where he was going because you stopped him before he got there.

It's the bucks we miss, or those whose tracks we puzzle over, that teach us something that might make us better hunters. I have learned more about deer behavior, about their travel routes and patterns, and about their preferred cover types under different weather conditions in those seasons where I never fired a shot, than I have in the seasons that ended abruptly and successfully in less than half a day.

I just hope I've learned enough over the years to take a buck on opening morning next season. (Dan)

Nana's Venison Meatballs

Sauce Ingredients:
2 cloves garlic, minced
1 medium onion, chopped
2 tablespoons olive oil
4 6-ounce cans tomato paste
1/4 teaspoon oregano
1 teaspoon fresh parsley, chopped

Meatball Ingredients:
1 pound ground venison
1/2 pound ground pork
1/2 cup bread crumbs
1/2 cup freshly grated Parmesan cheese
1 small onion, chopped
1/4 cup fresh parsley, chopped
4 large eggs

Sauté garlic and onion in oil until soft. Add tomato paste and 12 cans water. Stir well. Bring to hard boil, turn down heat and simmer 1-1/2 hours, stirring frequently. Add oregano and parsley. Continue to simmer while you make meatballs.

Mix all meatball ingredients together. Wet hands (so meat doesn't stick) and make meatballs. Add them to the simmering sauce and simmer covered for 30 minutes.

If the sauce has too much acid flavor, add 1/4 teaspoon sugar and stir. Repeat if needed.

Variation: Simmer meatballs for 6 to 8 hours in sauce made from 20 ounces ketchup and 10 ounces apple jelly. Ideal for crock pot!
4 servings
Serve with boiled potatoes sprinkled with parsley.

Boiled and Sliced Venison Heart for Sandwiches

1 deer heart
2 bay leaves
salt and pepper
1 small onion, quartered

Place heart in a large saucepan and add enough water to cover. Add remaining ingredients. Bring to a boil, turn down heat, cover and simmer for 2 to 3 hours or until heart is tender. Remove heart, drain and cool. Store overnight in refrigerator. Slice very thinly. Serve on whole-wheat bread with hot mustard or lettuce and mayonnaise.

GRILLED VENISON TERIYAKI

1 pound venison steak

3 tablespoons brown sugar

3 garlic cloves, minced, or 1 teaspoon garlic powder

1 tablespoon grated fresh ginger root or 1/8 teaspoon ginger powder

1/2 cup vegetable oil

1 cup soy sauce

2 tablespoons sherry wine

Slice venison steak into 1 inch strips and remove all visible fat. Combine all ingredients in a bowl and marinate steak in the refrigerator for 4 to 12 hours. Turn the meat occasionally. Grill or broil marinated meat for a couple of minutes on each side.

VENISON AND POTATO SAUSAGE

10 pounds ground lean venison

10 pounds ground raw potato

3 pounds ground raw onion

10 teaspoons salt

5 teaspoons pepper

sausage casings

Mix all ingredients and put through meat grinder. Fill sausage casings by hand or with a sausage stuffer attachment on your meat grinder. Tie off or twist sausage into individual links or leave whole as desired. Do not pack casings too tightly or they will burst when cooked. Wrap in meal-size packages and freeze. Sausage will keep for up to a year in the freezer.

To serve, punch a few holes in the frozen casing to prevent bursting and boil for 45 minutes. Leftovers may be served hot or cold.

Variation: Add 3 pounds ground pork and an additional 3 pounds of ground raw potatoes, 3 teaspoons salt and 1-1/2 teaspoons pepper to above recipe. The addition of pork to the recipe reduces freezer storage time to about 3 months.

CANNED VENISON

venison, chunked, approximately 1 pound per jar

1 or 2 bay leaves

1 teaspoon salt

1 small onion, quartered

Kitchen Bouquet

Pack raw venison into wide mouth quart jars and fill 3/4 full with water. Run a knife down the sides to expel all air bubbles. Add bay leaves, salt and onion in the above proportions to each jar. Pressure cook at 15 pounds pressure for 90 minutes.

To serve, drain juice into a saucepan. Add a few drops of Kitchen Bouquet for richer color, thicken sauce and add chunks of venison. Heat and serve.

How many times have you heard a deer hunter say, "I sat for two hours without seeing a thing. Then all of a sudden, there he was, standing right in the open. I don't know where he came from or how long he had been standing there looking at me, but when I reached for my rifle, he just disappeared!"

The monotony of deer hunting, especially stand hunting, can dull the senses. For the first hour, your senses are tuned in to everything that goes on around your stand. You notice the flicker of every leaf or strip of birch bark stirred by the slightest breeze. Your ears pick up the tapping of every woodpecker, every squirrel rustling in the fallen leaves.

As the hours pass, you glass again and again the patch of hazel brush with the profile of an eight-pointer, or that log you could have sworn was a bedded deer's rump. Then, slowly but surely your eyes glaze over, your ears ignore the fiftieth chickadee or nuthatch that lands in the tree behind you, your mind wanders to a hot shower and dinner.

And then you snap out of your reverie, and the buck is there. He could not possibly have come this close without your seeing him, but he has and you are taken totally by surprise. (Dan)

A whitetail buck's antlers are fascinating appendages. They grow from pedicels on top of the skull and are solid bone. The size and shape of a buck's antlers are determined by heredity and affected by nutritional factors, such as available minerals in the soil, food abundance and the severity of the previous winter.

Deer shed their antlers each winter and grow new ones in spring. The tender new antlers are covered with a pulpy skin called "velvet", which contains a layer of blood vessels that nourish them. By late August or early September, the antlers are fully developed and the velvet dries up and begins to fall off.

In the fall, bucks often "attack" brush and shrubs with their antlers and use them to rub the bark off small trees. These "rubs" announce "buck here" to other deer and to astute hunters who look for these unmistakable signposts.

Prior to and during the rut, bucks often spar with each other to establish dominance for breeding. Occasionally, two big bucks will lock antlers in a fight that can end in the death of both deer.

You can't tell a buck's exact age by examining his antlers, but if you are lucky enough to find the shed antlers of the same deer several years in a row, you'll see that they develop in a similar pattern from year to year. Look for shed antlers in late winter and early spring in areas where deer yard up for the winter. Relatively few sheds are ever found because mice and other rodents actually eat them for the minerals they contain. (Dan)

"The sheep's in the meadow, the deer's in the corn..."

In farm country, deer often spend a great deal of time in standing corn. Unpicked corn provides them with both food and cover, so there is little need for deer to leave it if they are unmolested.

A solitary bowhunter can get surprisingly close shots at unsuspecting deer in cornfields. Choose a windy day and enter the cornfield about 40 yards from the end on the downwind side, at right angles to the rows. Look both ways down each row before you step into it, moving slowly across the field. When you reach the other side of the field, move down 40 yards past where you could see and walk back the other way.

Deer walk, stand and bed parallel to corn rows, so there's a 50-50 chance a deer you see will be looking the other way. When you spot one that hasn't seen you, back up four rows and walk slowly toward it. You'll probably spook at least half the deer you try to "cornstalk," but with a little practice you'll find it's relatively easy to approach close enough for a point-blank shot.

"Cornstalking" may not have the aesthetic appeal of a northwoods deer hunt, but to see deer you have to go where they are. In agricultural areas, where they are is often in the corn. (Dan)

PRESSURE COOKED VENISON STEAKS

6 venison round steaks
3 tablespoons flour
1 teaspoon salt
1/2 teaspoon marjoram
2 tablespoons vegetable oil
1 small peeled onion
4 medium carrots, scraped
1/2 cup diced celery and tops
1-1/2 cups beef broth

Dredge steaks in flour mixed with salt and marjoram. Brown in oil in pressure pan. Add remaining ingredients, cover and cook at 10 pounds of pressure for 20 to 30 minutes after pressure guage jiggles. Cool closed for 5 minutes, then put under cold water to decrease pressure quickly. Mash vegetables and return to gravy to thicken it.
6 servings

VENISON SLOPPY JOES

3 pounds ground venison
1/4 cup butter
1 teaspoon garlic powder
1 teaspoon salt
1/2 teaspoon pepper
1 tablespoon soy sauce
1 tablespoon Worcestershire sauce
1 medium onion, chopped
1/2 cup celery, chopped
1 10-1/2 ounce can cream of mushroom or cream of celery soup

Melt butter in a large skillet. Add venison, garlic powder, salt, pepper, soy sauce and Worcestershire; brown lightly. Add onion and celery and cook until tender. Add soup. Simmer 30 minutes. Serve on rice, noodles or in hamburger buns.
10 to 12 servings

BARBECUED VENISON RIBS

Cut venison ribs into sections of 3 to 4 ribs each
(Allow 1 to 2 sections per person)

SAUCE:

1 cup chili sauce

1-1/2 cups water

1/2 cup Worcestershire sauce

2 tablespoons lemon juice

1/2 teaspoon salt

1 teaspoon cornstarch dissolved in water

chili powder to taste

   Combine ingredients for sauce, except cornstarch, in a small saucepan. Bring to a boil, then simmer 5 minutes. Slowly add cornstarch to thicken. Remove from heat.
   Place ribs on a rack with a shallow pan or foil to catch drippings. Roast at 400° for 10 to 20 minutes to remove excess tallow. Transfer ribs to a foil-lined roasting pan and baste liberally with barbecue sauce. Reduce heat to 350° and roast ribs, basting and turning frequently, until tender.
   Serve with a baked potato and a crisp garden salad.

Dan's son Jonathan will trade venison steaks for barbecued ribs any day — it's his all-time favorite recipe. Dan used to bone out the ribs, then wonder what to do with all the tallow and shreds of meat he ended up with. Then he discovered a recipe for ribs, and has never boned a rib since.
   We have modified this recipe over the years, but there's no reason you can't still improve upon it. If your deer is especially fat, you'll want to trim some tallow off the ribs before freezing them. An alternative is to broil the ribs for awhile, to melt off excess tallow, before you barbecue them. (Nancy)

CAMP VENISON

2 pounds venison, cut in pieces

1/2 cup flour

1 teaspoon salt

1 teaspoon pepper

1/4 teaspoon garlic salt

2 tablespoons vegetable oil

4 large onions

1 tablespoon Worcestershire sauce

1 large can tomatoes (do not drain)

1 10-1/2 ounce can cream of mushroom soup

Combine flour, salt, pepper and garlic salt in a large plastic bag. Add venison and shake to coat all pieces. Brown. Add onions and Worcestershire. Simmer 5 minutes and add tomatoes with juice and soup. Simmer for 1-1/2 hours. Serve on noodles or on mashed potatoes.

6 to 8 servings

A gelatin mold fruit salad makes an excellent side dish.

SAVORY VENISON STEW

2 pounds boneless venison stew meat cut in 1inch cubes

1/4 cup bacon drippings

1/2 cup flour

2 to 3 medium onions, coarsely chopped

3 to 4 carrots, sliced

2 to 3 stalks of celery, coarsely chopped

2 cans beef broth (10-1/2 ounces), or 20 ounces homemade
    game stock

1 to 2 cups dry red wine (enough to cover vegetables)

2 bay leaves, crushed

salt and pepper to taste

Rub bottom and sides of Dutch oven or large pot with bacon drippings to prevent sticking. Add vegetables, salt and pepper to taste, cover and cook slowly over low heat.

Dredge meat chunks lightly in flour and brown them in bacon drippings in a large skillet. When browned, add to vegetables.

Add stock and enough red wine to cover ingredients. Sprinkle with crushed bay leaves, stir, and cover. Simmer over low heat for 2 hours. Stir occasionally to prevent sticking. Serve over rice or hot biscuits.

4 to 5 servings

BARBECUED VENISON STEAK SANDWICHES

2 pounds venison round steak or roast, cut in slices

2 tablespoons vegetable oil

1 teaspoon salt

1/2 teaspoon pepper

1 teaspoon chili powder

2 sliced onions

2 tablespoons vinegar

1 tablespoon Worcestershire sauce

3/4 cup catsup

flour and water to thicken gravy

Brown venison on both sides. Place in Dutch oven and pour rest of ingredients over meat. Add enough water to cover. Cover and bake 2 hours at 350°. Thicken juice for gravy. Serve on toasted buns.

8 servings

GRILLED STEAK MARINADE

1-1/2 to 2 pounds venison steaks

1 teaspoon garlic salt

1-1/2 teaspoon ground ginger

1 green onion, chopped

3/4 cup oil

1/4 cup soy sauce

3 tablespoons honey

2 tablespoons red wine vinegar

button or honey mushrooms

Mix all ingredients except venison and mushrooms. Pour marinade over steak which has been placed in a shallow pan. Cover with plastic wrap directly on surface of meat to seal out air. Let stand in refrigerator 5 to 10 hours, turning several times. The longer the time, the more tender and tasty the venison will be. Grill over coals or gas grill as you would your favorite steak. Do not overcook. Slice in thin diagonal slices across the grain. Serve with button or honey mushrooms in heated marinade which has had most of the oil poured off before heating.

3 to 4 servings

Dutch Oven Steaks

1-1/2 pounds venison steak

4 tablespoons cornstarch

1/2 teaspoon salt

1/2 teaspoon pepper

1 tablespoon dry mustard

2 tablespoons vegetable shortening

4 large onions, diced

1 carrot, diced

1 large can tomatoes, drained

Combine cornstarch, salt, pepper and mustard. Pound into steaks with meat tenderizer. Brown in very hot grease in a Dutch oven. Cover with onions, carrots and tomatoes. Bake for 1-1/2 hours at 300°. Serve with fried or baked potatoes.

2 servings

Wild foods are a valuable resource and one that deserves to be treated with as much respect in the kitchen as in the field. The gentle preparation of properly handled fish, game and other wild foods will yield culinary delights tempting enough to pique the most jaded appetite and refined enough to please the most discriminating palate.

Unlike many commercially available foods, wild foods are not uniform. When we buy frying chicken or a young hen turkey, we know what to expect, but no two mallards or deer are exactly the same. Each recipe will produce satisfactory results if used as a general guide, not as an exact prescription. Only you know how you like your meals to taste and look, and which spices you like.

VENISON LIVER

1/4 to 1/2 pound venison liver per person, sliced very thinly

flour

salt and pepper

3 tablespoons butter or bacon fat

2 medium onions, sliced and separated into rings

Dredge liver slices in flour seasoned with salt and pepper. Melt 3 tablespoons of butter in a large skillet. Add the onion rings and sauté them over medium heat until tender. Move onions to the side of the pan and sauté the liver slices in the same butter for 2 minutes, 1 minute per side. Serve liver slices topped with onion rings on a heated platter.

Bacon served on the side complements liver flavor.

Venison liver is best when it is fresh. I try to eat mine within a couple days, rather than freeze it. Liver makes a great deer camp meal. It is easy to prepare, and it lets you taste the rewards of the hunt the very day you bag a deer.

For variety, fry up some bacon and substitute bacon drippings for butter, then garnish the liver with bacon strips. (Dan)

BRAISED VENISON CHOPS

4 venison chops

flour

salt and pepper

2 tablespoons shortening

1 cup Burgundy or claret wine

1 small can mushrooms

Roll chops in flour well-seasoned with salt and pepper. Brown well in shortening. Add 1/2 cup water and simmer until tender. Pour wine over chops and cook down until almost dry. Drain mushrooms, reserving liquid. Add 3/4 teaspoon cornstarch to mushroom liquid and add enough water to make 1/2 cup. Remove chops to platter. Stir liquid and cornstarch in the pan until it reaches gravy consistency. Add mushrooms. Pour gravy over chops.

Serve with asparagus spears smothered in hollandaise sauce.

ITALIAN VENISON CHIPS

1/2 pound venison chips (slices approximately 2 inches in
     diameter and 1/4 inch thick)

3/4 cup olive oil

1-1/2 teaspoons rosemary

3 garlic cloves, crushed

1 bunch green onions, chopped

1 bunch fresh parsley, chopped

Burgundy wine

Marinate venison chips in olive oil, rosemary and crushed garlic overnight or for at least 2 to 3 hours. Sauté meat quickly in a little olive oil; throw in a handful of onion and parsley. Cover the meat with Burgundy wine and bring to an easy boil. Serve immediately.

Meat from any large muscle will work in this recipe, if chips are cut across the grain, but loin is best and easiest to work with.

Carrots, steamed and glazed, served on the side, add counterpoint to the Burgundy marinade.

DAN'S INCOMPARABLE VENISON SPAGHETTI SAUCE

1 pound ground venison

2 tablespoons vegetable oil (optional)

2 15-ounce cans tomato sauce

1 4-ounce can mushrooms, drained

1/4 cup green olives, chopped

1 tablespoon Worcestershire sauce

sage, rosemary, thyme, basil, oregano, savory, marjoram to taste

Brown venison in large non-stick skillet, use 2 tablespoons vegetable oil if skillet is not of a non-stick variety. Transfer to large saucepan. Add two cans tomato sauce and stir as you bring to a boil. Add mushrooms. Turn down heat; simmer and add spices to taste. Stir. Cover and simmer 45 minutes to 1 hour. Stir occasionally and taste. Add more spices if necessary. Serve over drained, cooked spaghetti. Freeze any leftover sauce—it always tastes better the second time.

Variation: For a little more zip, add one clove of fresh garlic, finely chopped, and one small onion, treated likewise. Toss these in with the venison when you brown it.

4 servings

VENISON LASAGNA

1 pound ground venison

3 teaspoons garlic powder

4 tablespoons dried parsley, chopped

1 tablespoon dried oregano

1-1/2 teaspoons dried basil leaves

2 teaspoons salt

1/8 teaspoon pepper

1/8 teaspoon cayenne

1 large onion, chopped

1 1-pound, 12-ounce can whole tomatoes, undrained

2 6-ounce cans tomato paste

8 lasagna noodles

24 ounces mozzarella cheese, grated

1 8-ounce containe ricotta cheese

1/2 cup grated Parmesan cheese

Brown venison in a large skillet. While browning, add onion, garlic, parsley, oregano, basil, salt, pepper and cayenne. Break tomatoes into small pieces and add with tomato paste. Simmer uncovered for about 30 minutes. Preheat oven to 350°. Cook lasagna according to package directions; rinse with hot water. Lightly grease a 13 x 9 inch baking pan. Layer 4 noodles, 1/2 mozzarella, 1/2 tomato/meat sauce, 1/2 ricotta. Repeat. Sprinkle Parmesan on top. Bake 30 to 35 minutes or until cheese is melted and lasagna is heated through. Let stand for approximately 5 minutes, cut and serve.

Hint: Double the tomato/meat sauce recipe and save half for spaghetti. It can be refrigerated for several days while the flavors blend further.

4 to 6 servings

VENISON STROGANOFF

1 pound venison stew meat cut across the grain in 1/4" slices

2 tablespoons bacon drippings

3 tablespoons butter

8 ounces sliced canned mushrooms or 1/2 pound fresh mushrooms

1 medium onion, finely chopped

1 clove garlic, minced

1 can (10-1/2 ounces) condensed beef broth

1 cup dairy sour cream

2 tablespoons dry white wine

flour

salt

Dredge meat in seasoned flour. Heat bacon drippings in skillet and brown meat quickly on both sides. Add mushrooms, onion and garlic. Stir and cook over medium heat 3 to 4 minutes. Remove ingredients to the top of a double boiler.

Add 2 tablespoons butter to drippings in skillet and stir in 3 tablespoons flour and beef broth. Cook over medium heat until the mixture thickens; then add to meat and mushrooms in double boiler.

Stir in sour cream and white wine and allow mixture to heat through. Just before serving, stir in 1 tablespoon butter and serve immediately over buttered noodles.

4 to 5 servings

It pays to be prepared for any type of weather during the gun deer season. Dressing for "typical" hunting weather—air temperatures in the upper twenties, light northwest winds, snow flurries—is no problem, but I can recall sitting through more than one sub-zero blizzard, and even a balmy Thanksgiving hunt when we wished we had blaze-orange T-shirts!

A deer hunter's least favorite weather is rain. A drizzle you can put up with, but a soaking downpour dampens everyone's enthusiasm for the hunt. Deer sometimes move in the rain, however, so when the clouds opened up on the first day of the season several years ago, I hurried back to camp, oiled my rifle, donned chest waders and a Gore-Tex jacket, then clambered back up into my tree.

While other hunters got wet and miserable, I remained dry and relatively comfortable. Raindrops pattered on the forest floor and wood frogs, roused prematurely from their muddy sleep by the warm rain, chorused as though it were April.

Just before noon that day, the best buck I had seen in years came skulking through the hardwoods. I killed him at fifty yards with a heart shot that silenced the wood frogs for only a moment before they resumed their croaking.

That night, in every northwoods laundromat, hunters glumly fed quarters to the slots as orange coats tumbled brightly behind the round, glass doors. (Dan)

VENISON JERKY

2-1/2 pounds venison cut into strips 1/2 inch on a side

1 tablespoon salt

1 tablespoon sugar

1 teaspoon onion powder

1/2 teaspoon pepper

Preheat oven to 140°. Spread venison evenly on ungreased baking sheets. Combine seasonings in a small bowl. Sprinkle over all sides of meat. Bake for about 4 hours, turning once, until dark brown and dried. Turn off oven and leave jerky in oven for 24 hours before storing in airtight plastic containers.

Good for packing along on most outings for a quick and tasty snack.

CHINESE VENISON PEPPER STEAK

1 pound venison stew meat, sliced across the grain, 1/4 inch slices

2 medium green peppers, sliced into thin Chinese-style slices

3 tablespoons peanut oil (other cooking oils may burn at
high temperature)

Marinade:

3 tablespoons dark soy sauce

2 tablespoons dry, white wine

2 tablespoons cornstarch

1 teaspoon sugar (not to sweeten, but to harmonize taste)

1/4 teaspoon pepper

Mix marinade ingredients in a bowl and add meat slices. Marinate for 45 minutes. Heat wok or large skillet and add 2 tablespoons oil. Stir-fry peppers until they are translucent. Do not overcook; they should remain crisp and bright green. Remove peppers to another bowl. Add 1 tablespoon oil to wok and stir-fry meat slices. Replace peppers in wok for 30 seconds. Serve immediately over a bed of steamed white rice. Add soy sauce to suit individual taste.

3 to 4 servings

The secret to making this recipe a stunning success is to use only the most tender cuts of venison. Loin or rump will produce excellent results, but if you really want to impress your guests, serve them tenderloin — their pepper steak will literally be fork-tender.

We have tried stir-fry recipes with stew meat from the shoulder or shank, but the cooking time is too short to break down the connective tissue, and the stuff is impossible to chew. The only way to salvage tough cuts of meat for a stir-fry dish is to marinate them at least overnight, if not longer. (Nancy)

Still-hunting can be an effective way to hunt whitetails, especially in areas where there are few hunters to move deer around. But still-hunting works only when you can use the wind, weather and terrain to your advantage. Your goal as a still hunter is to blend in with the natural sounds and movements of the woods, and to see deer before they sense your presence.

Of the three senses deer rely on to warn them of danger, hearing and smell are the most acute. A deer's eyesight, on the other hand, isn't much better than yours.

On calm, dry days when falling leaves crunch underfoot like cornflakes, you'd be better off taking a stand and waiting for deer to come to you. Similarly, if you hunt downwind, a deer will often smell you long before you can approach close enough for a shot. Choose a day when a light rain or snowfall quiets your footsteps, and when a steady, light breeze is blowing. Enter the woods upwind or crosswind, and move very slowly, stopping every few yards for several minutes before moving on. Scan the cover ahead and to the side, looking for parts, not the whole deer—a patch of white throat hair, the flick of an ear or tail, the horizontal line of the deer's back

Still-hunting presents more of a challenge than other forms of deer hunting, but the exhilaration of outsmarting a buck using this one-on-one technique will keep you going for many seasons to come. (Dan)

VENISON AND ONION STEW

3 pounds boneless venison pot roast, cut into 1/2 inch slices

2 tablespoons butter

6 medium onions, chopped

1/2 teaspoon flour

1 teaspoon sugar

1/4 cup broth

1 cup light beer

1/2 teaspoon salt

1/4 teaspoon pepper

1 bay leaf

Brown meat in butter in a large, heavy skillet or Dutch oven. Remove meat and brown onions lightly in the same pan. Add flour and sugar and cook until browned. Add broth and beer and bring to a boil. Return meat to the pan add remaining ingredients. Cover tightly and simmer for 3 hours or until meat is tender. Remove bay leaf. Serve with noodles, rice or potatoes.

10 to 12 servings

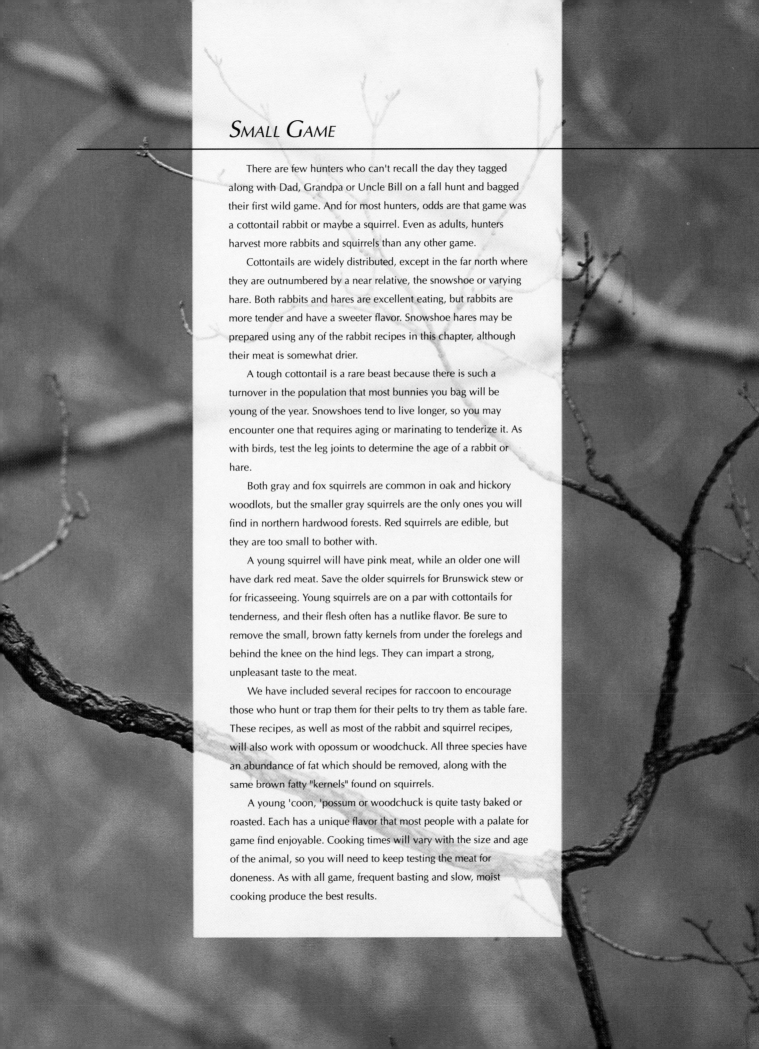

SMALL GAME

There are few hunters who can't recall the day they tagged along with Dad, Grandpa or Uncle Bill on a fall hunt and bagged their first wild game. And for most hunters, odds are that game was a cottontail rabbit or maybe a squirrel. Even as adults, hunters harvest more rabbits and squirrels than any other game.

Cottontails are widely distributed, except in the far north where they are outnumbered by a near relative, the snowshoe or varying hare. Both rabbits and hares are excellent eating, but rabbits are more tender and have a sweeter flavor. Snowshoe hares may be prepared using any of the rabbit recipes in this chapter, although their meat is somewhat drier.

A tough cottontail is a rare beast because there is such a turnover in the population that most bunnies you bag will be young of the year. Snowshoes tend to live longer, so you may encounter one that requires aging or marinating to tenderize it. As with birds, test the leg joints to determine the age of a rabbit or hare.

Both gray and fox squirrels are common in oak and hickory woodlots, but the smaller gray squirrels are the only ones you will find in northern hardwood forests. Red squirrels are edible, but they are too small to bother with.

A young squirrel will have pink meat, while an older one will have dark red meat. Save the older squirrels for Brunswick stew or for fricasseeing. Young squirrels are on a par with cottontails for tenderness, and their flesh often has a nutlike flavor. Be sure to remove the small, brown fatty kernels from under the forelegs and behind the knee on the hind legs. They can impart a strong, unpleasant taste to the meat.

We have included several recipes for raccoon to encourage those who hunt or trap them for their pelts to try them as table fare. These recipes, as well as most of the rabbit and squirrel recipes, will also work with opossum or woodchuck. All three species have an abundance of fat which should be removed, along with the same brown fatty "kernels" found on squirrels.

A young 'coon, 'possum or woodchuck is quite tasty baked or roasted. Each has a unique flavor that most people with a palate for game find enjoyable. Cooking times will vary with the size and age of the animal, so you will need to keep testing the meat for doneness. As with all game, frequent basting and slow, moist cooking produce the best results.

BUTTERMILK RABBIT

1 rabbit
1-1/2 cups bread crumbs
1/2 stick butter or margarine
2 cups buttermilk
3 strips bacon
paprika, salt and pepper

Cut rabbit into pieces as you would a chicken, but cut the back into two pieces. Melt butter or margarine. Dip rabbit pieces in melted butter; then roll in bread crumbs until evenly coated. Place rabbit pieces in a buttered casserole dish and cover with some of the bread crumbs left after coating rabbit. Lightly salt and pepper. Cover rabbit and crumbs with buttermilk. Top with bacon, and garnish with paprika. Bake at 350° for 1 to 1-1/2 hours, or until rabbit is tender
3 to 4 servings
Serve with a baked potato and buttered carrots.

Bunnies and beagles go together like bourbon and branch, but don't sit home and mope if you don't own a hound, because a dogless hunter can still have plenty of fun chasing rabbits.

If you hunt with a partner and there is snow on the ground, you can take turns playing hound and hunter. The hunter waits in a strategic location—on top of a railroad grade or near where several game trails cross—while the "hound" pushes through thickets to get the rabbits moving. If the snow is fresh enough, the "hound" partner can often follow a rabbit's tracks through the tangles and dog the bunny right to the waiting shooter.

If you're hunting alone, try jumping rabbits from cover. Brush piles, fallen logs, derelict farm machinery and back-forty junkpiles are good places to try. Rabbits will often sit tight if the cover keeps them out of sight avian predators, so you may need to literally kick them out of hiding. In more open cover, a slow, walk-stop-walk-stop pace will usually unnerve rabbits and flush them within gun range.

Whether you pursue them with a pack of baying hounds, or alone with just the sound of snow crunching beneath your boots, a cottontail hunt is an exciting way to spend a sunny winter afternoon and a fine way to provide some of the tastiest, most tender wild meat for the table. (Dan)

LEMON RABBIT

1 rabbit, cut into serving pieces
flour
1 tablespoon olive oil
1 tablespoon butter
1 medium onion, chopped
3 lemons, sliced
2 cups chicken stock
1/2 teaspoon thyme
3 large sprigs fresh parsley
1 bay leaf
salt and pepper to taste
chopped fresh parsley for garnish

Pat rabbit dry with paper towels. Dredge in flour. Lightly brown rabbit pieces in oil and butter in a stove-top casserole. Remove. Brown the onions in remaining butter and oil. Remove. Arrange a layer of lemon slices in the bottom of the casserole. Add rabbit and onions. Add seasonings. Arrange remaining lemons on the top.

Pour stock over ingredients to barely cover. Cover casserole and simmer for 20 to 30 minutes. Stock should be sauce consistency. Vary by uncovering to evaporate, or adding stock, depending on thickness.

Garnish with parsley and serve with rice.

3 to 4 servings

As a side dish, serve steamed artichokes with a hollandaise sauce.

SLOW COOKER RABBIT IN WINE

1 or 2 rabbits, cut into serving pieces
1/2 cup red wine
2 teaspoons minced onion
1 cup dairy sour cream
1 can cream of mushroom soup (10-1/2 oz.)
1/4 teaspoon Worcestershire sauce
salt and pepper to taste
paprika

Layer rabbit pieces in slow cooker, seasoning lightly with salt, pepper and paprika between layers. Mix wine, soup, sour cream, Worcestershire and onion until well combined. Pour over rabbit and cook on low heat 7 to 8 hours.

Serve over buttered noodles, accompanied by a tossed green salad.

4 to 6 servings

HASSENPFEFFER

1 large rabbit, cut into serving
  pieces

3/4 cup cider vinegar

1-1/2 cups water

1 teaspoon whole cloves

3 bay leaves

2 teaspoons salt

1/4 teaspoon pepper

2 teaspoons sugar

1 medium onion, sliced

3 tablespoons butter

1 teaspoon Worcestershire sauce

1/8 teaspoon allspice

1/4 cup flour

gingersnaps (optional)

Combine vinegar, water, spices, seasonings and onion. Marinate rabbit pieces in a covered crock or glass bowl in the refrigerator for at least 12 hours (preferably 1 to 1-1/2 days). Remove rabbit and drain well. Coat pieces in flour and brown well in hot butter or shortening. Remove excess fat and add marinating liquid. Cover and simmer 1 hour (2 hours for mature rabbit) or until tender. Remove rabbit meat to hot platter. Thicken liquid for gravy with flour or finely crushed gingersnaps.
  4 to 6 servings

CREOLE RABBIT

2 rabbits, cut into 6
  pieces each

1/2 cup flour

1-1/2 teaspoon salt

1/4 teaspoon pepper

1/4 cup butter or oil

Creole Sauce:

2 medium onions, sliced

1 clove garlic, minced

1-1/2 tablespoons parsley, chopped

3 tablespoons butter or oil

3-1/2 cups tomato juice

1/2 teaspoon Worcestershire sauce

salt and pepper

Cook onions, garlic and parsley in butter or oil until onion is golden brown. Add tomato juice and Worcestershire sauce and simmer for 15 minutes. Add salt and pepper to taste.
  Coat moist pieces of rabbit in flour, salt and pepper by shaking together in a paper bag. Heat butter or oil in a heavy skillet and lightly brown rabbit on all sides. Put rabbit in a casserole dish; pour sauce over rabbit, cover and bake at 325° for 1 hour or until tender.
  3 to 4 servings

RABBIT PIE

2 pounds rabbit pieces

1 pound stewing beef or venison

1 cup flour

shortening

1 teaspoon salt

1/2 teaspoon pepper

1 large onion, chopped

3 carrots, chopped

3 medium potatoes

1/4 cup flour

1/3 cup water

salt and pepper to taste

standard recipe for pastry crust

Dredge rabbit pieces and pieces of red meat in flour and brown in 1/4 inch of hot shortening in Dutch oven. Remove excess oil and add boiling water to cover meat. Add salt, pepper and onion. Cover and simmer 1 hour. Add vegetables. Simmer 1/2 hour or until tender. Remove meat and vegetables from broth. Remove meat from bones. Dice meat. Thicken 2 cups of broth with 1/4 cup flour mixed with 1/3 cup water. Season to taste. Put meat and vegetables in a large casserole and add thickened broth to cover. Make pastry dough and roll 1/2 inch larger than casserole. Place pastry over hot meat sauce and slit center. Turn edge under and flute. Bake pie at 450° for 20 minutes or until crust is golden.

6 servings

An avocado salad makes a delicious accompaniment to this hearty meal.

We taped a cottontail rabbit hunt with Jim Kalkofen and Dic Schultz that worked out so well we decided to quit while we were ahead, and haven't hunted cottontails on TV since.

Jim and Dic took us to a spruce grove isolated on this January day from other nearby cover by snow-covered fields. They placed me near one end of the narrow grove, about 20 yards from an old shed, and told me the rabbits (note the plural) would run to the end of the cover, then either double back or duck under the shed. Then Jim took their three beagles around to the other end of the spruce grove and turned them loose.

I hunted cottontails with beagles for years in my youth, but rarely had the bunnies done what I expected them to, so I watched these two escape routes with growing skepticism. The baying hounds drew nearer, then a cottontail appeared and—you guessed it—ran right under the shed!

I suddenly became a believer and watched eagerly for another rabbit, trying to forget the chance I had blown. The next one came running along the same path as the first, and I rolled it just before it reached the shed. A third rabbit got by us in the commotion and joined the first one under the shed, then one of them decided it was getting crowded under there and raced back out, right past Dic who managed to bag it. All this with the camera rolling, mind you!

After that flurry of action, Dic took me to the end of a second spruce grove and had me stand on a wide trail that ran alongside the trees, while Jim and my son Jonathan waited at the other end with the hounds.

"Jim will bring the dogs through the spruce and push the rabbits to us," Dic told me. "They usually come out right there and cross the trail," he said, pointing to the corner of the grove.

This time I was ready when a cottontail hopped out right where Dic had indicated. I shot it just as it crossed the trail, and again, we caught the scene on tape. We ended the segment by presenting Jim with one of the three rabbits, since he had done such a fine job of choreographing both dogs and cottontails. (Dan)

ROAST SQUIRREL

1 squirrel per person
1-1/2 teaspoons salt
1/4 tablespoon lemon juice or tarragon vinegar
1/4 cup butter, melted, or 2 tablespoons butter and 2 tablespoons oil
1 cup beef broth

Multiply all ingredients by the number of squirrels used. Sprinkle squirrel with salt and pepper. Mix lemon juice and oil and brush on squirrel. Place on a rack in a Dutch oven. Add broth, cover and roast at 325° for 1-1/2 hours. Cover can be removed for the last 30 minutes for browning. If desired, make gravy from pan drippings.
This is a good way to cook an older, less tender squirrel.
Sauté julienned celery and zucchini for your vegetable side dish.

Our great luck with Jim Kalkofen and the rabbits led us to try a squirrel hunt with him the next winter. I was planning, any day, to pick up the new Jeep I had ordered, so I drove my old hunting car on what I thought might be its last outing. That thought turned out to be more prophetic than I guessed at the time.

Jim and I started hunting early in the morning, hoping to bag a squirrel or two before the camera crew joined us, but hadn't fired a shot when they pulled up mid-morning. They had shot plenty of footage of squirrels cavorting in a park on the way to meet us, however, so now all we needed was to shoot a squirrel or two with the .22s.

It took us the rest of the day, but we managed to get one squirrel apiece and demonstrate two styles of hunting in the process: Calling squirrels while hunting alone from tree stands, and working as a team to make treed squirrels show themselves long enough to get a shot at them.

When we taped the tree stand portion of the hunt, Jim jokingly called me a name we couldn't use on the air. My laughter was so spontaneous and the scene worked so well, we later decided to run it anyway, so Jim became the first person we ever had to "bleep" on OUTDOOR WISCONSIN.

That day went almost as smoothly as the rabbit hunt, and I was more than satisfied when we parted company late that afternoon. On the way home, however, my car's drive shaft snapped in two, cracking the transmission housing and leaving me stranded miles from home and only days from a new Jeep. Now, you don't suppose that old buggy was trying to tell me something, do you? (Dan)

SQUIRREL WRAPPED IN BACON

2 to 3 squirrels, each cut into 5 pieces

10 to 15 slices bacon

3 to 4 cups wild rice, cooked, or long grain or instant

5 large carrots, cut lengthwise

5 stalks celery, cut up

2 tablespoons butter

dash of garlic salt

dash of red pepper, crushed

Wrap the squirrel sections with pieces of bacon and secure with round toothpicks. Butter the sides and bottom of a medium roasting pan and add a small amount of water to keep the ingredients from sticking. Spread about 3/4 of the cooked rice in the pan. Arrange pieces of carrots and celery on the rice. Press the bacon-wrapped squirrel sections into the rice and mound the remaining rice around the meat. Sprinkle with a dash of garlic salt and a dash of crushed red pepper. Bake at 325° to 350° for 2 to 3 hours or until done.

3 to 4 servings

BRUNSWICK STEW

2 squirrels, cut into serving pieces

1 quart boiling water

1 cup corn, canned or frozen

1 cup lima beans, canned or frozen

2 medium potatoes, peeled and cubed

2 cups tomatoes, fresh or canned

1 small onion, quartered

1/4 cup butter

salt and pepper

Boil one quart salted water or liquid drained from canned vegetables in small stewpot. Add squirrel pieces and lower heat to simmer. Add vegetables, salt and pepper to taste. Cover and simmer for 1 hour. Add butter, stir and bring to a boil. Remove from heat and serve over hot biscuits.

2 to 3 servings

HUNTER STEW

2 to 3 pounds rabbit or squirrel
1/4 cup shortening
3 cups boiling water
3 medium potatoes, diced
3 medium carrots, diced
1/2 cup celery, sliced
1/4 cup parsley, chopped

1 medium onion, slicecd
2 teaspoons salt
1/4 teaspoon oregano
1/4 teaspoon savory
1/4 teaspoon pepper
1/4 cup flour
1/2 cup cold water

Brown rabbit in shortening in Dutch oven. Add water, cover and simmer for 30 minutes or until almost tender. Add potatoes, carrots, celery, parsley, onion and seasonings. Cook until vegetables are tender, about 20 minutes. Add flour to cold water to form a paste; stir into stew. Cook until slightly thickened. If desired, steam dumplings with stew.
4 to 6 servings

SQUIRREL FRICASSEE

1 young squirrel per person, cut in pieces
1/2 teaspoon salt
1/8 teaspoon pepper
1/2 cup flour
3 slices bacon, chopped
1 tablespoon sliced onion
2 teaspoons lemon juice
1/3 cup beef or chicken broth

Sprinkle meat with salt and pepper and coat with flour. Pan fry with bacon until well browned. Add remaining ingredients and cook slowly for 2 hours. Remove squirrel and use pan drippings to make a gravy by adding water or milk and flour, stirring over low heat until thickened.
Variation: Replace bacon and lemon juice with 2 tablespoons cooking oil, 1 tablespoon paprika, 1/8 teaspoon cayenne pepper, 1 tart apple and 2 cups of broth.
Let a side dish of green beans and pearl onions accompany your fricassee.
2 servings

STOVE-TOP BARBECUED RACCOON

1 raccoon
2 onions, sliced
black pepper
salt

Sauce Ingredients:
1/2 cup catsup
1-1/2 teaspoon salt
1/4 teaspoon Tabasco sauce
1/8 teaspoon chili powder
1 cup water
1/2 teaspoon ground mustard
1 tablespoon brown sugar

Cut raccoon into serving-sized pieces. Soak meat in salt water, 3 teaspoons per quart, for a minimum of 4 hours (or overnight in the refrigerator). Layer meat in large covered skillet alternating with layers of onions. Sprinkle with black pepper to taste. Mix all sauce ingredients together and pour over meat mixture. Cover and simmer over low heat until meat is tender.

4 to 6 servings

Cream sauce over cauliflower will set off this recipe.

BOARDING HOUSE ROAST RACCOON

3 to 4 raccoons, 4 to 6
    pounds each
5 tablespoons salt
2 teaspoons pepper
2 cups flour
1 cup shortening
8 medium onions, peeled
12 small bay leaves

Stuffing Ingredients:
3 loaves of day-old bread, crumbed
2-1/2 teaspoons salt
1 teaspoon pepper
2-1/2 teaspoons powdered sage
4 eggs, beaten
1 1-1/2 ounce envelope
    dehydrated onion soup
4 stalks celery, chopped
1/2 cup butter or margarine
4 cups raccoon broth

Skin, draw and clean raccoons soon after killing. Remove the brown bean-shaped kernels from under forelegs and each thigh without breaking them. Cut meat into pieces. Simmer the bony pieces in water with a little seasoning until tender. Strain and use the broth for gravy and dressing.

Season the meaty back and leg pieces with salt and pepper; coat with flour. Brown meat on all sides in shortening in a heavy skillet. Place pieces in a roaster, add onions and bay leaves. Cover and bake at 350° for about 3 hours or until tender.

Add 2 to 3 tablespoons flour for each cup of liquid drippings or added broth in the pan to make a gravy.

Mix all stuffing ingredients together. Bake in shallow pan at 350° for 30 minutes.

24 servings

A big steaming bowl of candied yams makes a tasty accompaniment to this hearty meal for a crowd.

FISH

Freshwater fish offer some of the best eating of any wild foods, and the great variety and availability of fish provide us with ample opportunity to sample the bounty of our lakes and streams. The secret to turning a creel of trout, a stringer of walleyes or a bucket of bluegills into an unforgettable meal, of course, is to keep the fish fresh and their preparation simple in the extreme.

Cooks and fishermen alike know this, but all too often those glistening beauties we traveled so far to catch end up drying out in the bottom of the boat or roasting in the truck on the long drive home. Put your catch on ice as soon as practically possible and clean them immediately upon returning home (after snapping the requisite trophy photos, of course).

Serve your family or guests pan-fried perch fillets, baked bass or grilled salmon steaks from fish that were whisked from lake, to ice, to kitchen and prepared the day, or day after, they were caught, and they will proclaim you a master chef. No need to tell them the flavor was there all along, and that you merely let it shine through with a simple recipe and a fresh fish.

BEER-BATTER WALLEYE

2 to 3 pounds walleye fillets

2 eggs, separated

1 cup flour

1 teaspoon salt

1/2 teaspoon garlic powder

1 can warm beer

3 tablespoons vegetable oil, divided

Beat egg whites until stiff. Beat flour, salt, garlic powder, beer, 2 teaspoons oil and egg yolks until smooth. Fold in egg whites. Dip fish, one at a time, in batter and fry in remaining oil heated to 375° in an electric fry pan. Fry 5 to 10 minutes or until golden brown on both sides.

4 to 6 servings

This recipe works well with a side dish of potato pancakes.

Walleyes are among the tastiest of all fish, and those taken from most waters are perfectly safe to eat. Tests of fish from some lakes and rivers, however, have revealed that certain fish—especially larger walleyes—contain unsafe levels of mercury contamination. Mercury occurs naturally in the environment, but it is also released in some industrial processes. Mercury can be especially harmful to pregnant women, nursing mothers and children. Twice each year, the Wisconsin DNR issues a health advisory that details the problem and lists lakes that contain species and sizes of fish that high-risk individuals should avoid eating.

Before eating fish from a body of water you are unfamiliar with, it is a good idea to consult the latest health advisory. In other states, check with the state DNR or Department of Health for similar information. (Dan)

OVEN-BAKED WALLEYE

6 serving-sized walleye fillets, 3/4 inch thick

1/2 cup mayonnaise

1 cup fresh bread crumbs

1/2 teaspoon of one of the following: rosemary, chervil or tarragon

1/3 cup melted butter

tartar sauce (optional)

lemon wedges (optional)

Place fillets in a shallow baking dish. Spread with mayonnaise. Combine bread crumbs and seasoning with melted butter. Spread on fillets. Bake about 30 minutes at 375°. Serve with tartar sauce and lemon.

GRILLED WALLEYE FILLETS IN CORN HUSKS

4 serving-sized walleye fillets

4 large ears corn

salt and pepper to taste

3 tablespoons chopped pimiento, drained

1 tablespoon fresh lemon juice

6 ounces mozzarella cheese, shredded

2 ounces feta cheese, finely crumbled

4 tablespoons butter

1 lemon, cut into wedges, for garnish

Carefully pull husks back from corn, leaving them attached to the stem. Remove silk and corn. Place husks in a large bowl with enough water to cover. Cut four foot-long pieces of cotton or linen string and soak with husks. Set aside. Salt and pepper fillets to taste. Mix pimiento and lemon juice. Remove husks from water and shake out the excess. Place one fillet in each husk, folding the fillet if necessary to make it fit. Top with both cheeses and pimento mixture; dot with butter. Close husks around fillet as if it were the ear of corn, being sure that fillet is totally enclosed. Tie ends tightly with string, cutting off the loose ends. Cook on the grill over medium heat for about 20 minutes, turning occasionally or until fish flakes easily. Serve in husks, garnished with lemon wedges.

BAKED WALLEYE FILLETS WITH CLAM STUFFING

2 pounds walleye fillets

1/4 cup onion, chopped

3 tablespoons butter

1 5-ounce can baby clams, drained and rinsed

2 cups soft bread cubes

1/2 teaspoon salt

1/8 teaspoon pepper

2 tablespoons parsley, chopped

2 tablespoons pimiento, chopped

1 10-ounce can cheddar cheese soup

1/4 cup fine, dry bread crumbs

1 tablespoon butter, melted

Sauté onion in butter until tender. Add clams, bread cubes, salt and pepper. Mix gently. Place half of fillets in a greased baking dish. Top with stuffing and cover with remaining fillets. Mix parsley, pimiento and soup; spoon over fish. Mix bread crumbs and butter; sprinkle on top. Bake for 25 minutes at 400° or until fish flakes easily.

The clam stuffing gives the familiar walleye an exotic taste your family or guests will find a refreshing change from the usual Friday night fish fry.

4 servings

FOILED FISH FILLETS

1/3 pound fish fillet per person

salt and pepper

Multiply all of the following ingredients by the number of
  fillets prepared:

1 tablespoon chopped green pepper

1 tablespoon chopped onion

3 tablespoons catsup

1 teaspoon butter, cut into small pieces

1 tablespoon Parmesan cheese

Place each fillet on a greased square of aluminum foil. Season with salt and pepper to taste. Top with all other ingredients. Seal fillets in foil and place on a cookie sheet. Bake for 20 minutes at 350°.

Try this recipe with your favorite fish. It's especially good with bass, northern pike or walleye.

CHEESY NORTHERN PIKE BAKE

1 northern pike, filleted, cut into serving-sized pieces
1 pound fresh broccoli
1 pound fresh cauliflower
1 teaspoon salt, divided
4 tablespoons butter, divided
2 tablespoons flour
1/8 teaspoon white pepper
1/8 teaspoon cayenne
1/8 teaspoon dry mustard
1 cup milk
1/4 cup cheddar cheese, shredded, divided
1/2 cup fine dry bread crumbs
1/8 teaspoon paprika

Separate broccoli into flowerets and cut stalks into 3/4 inch slices; prepare cauliflower the same way. Boil 1 quart of water with 1/2 teaspoon of salt in a 3 quart saucepan. Add broccoli and cauliflower, cover and cook for 5 minutes. Drain. Rinse in cold water; set aside. Melt 2 tablespoons butter in a 1 quart saucepan, stir in flour, salt, pepper, cayenne and mustard. Blend in milk. Cook over medium heat until bubbly and thickened. Stir in 1/4 cup cheese; set aside. Place vegetables in a greased 9 x 13 inch pan and spread with half of the cheese. Arrange northern fillets on top, add remaining cheese and pour on sauce. Set aside. Mix remaining 2 tablespoons butter, bread crumbs and paprika; sprinkle over top of fish. Bake 25 to 30 minutes at 350° or until fish flakes easily.

4 to 6 servings

You have perhaps noticed an absence of recipes for muskellunge. We love to catch muskies, but encourage you to release them. If you do happen to injure one so badly that it can't be released, any recipe for northern will work for muskies. Sadly, we had to kill one muskie last year, but it did not die in vain. I filleted it, removed the "Y" bones and cut the fillets into serving-size pieces. Broiled in lemon butter, they were flaky and delicious. (Dan)

Baked Northern With Cornbread Stuffing

1 4 to 6 pound fresh northern pike

2 cups cornbread stuffing, prepackaged, or crumbled cornbread
    or cornmeal muffins

1 tablespoon parsley flakes

1/2 teaspoon dill

salt and pepper

1/4 cup onion, chopped

1/4 cup celery, chopped

1-1/4 cup chicken broth

2 tablespoons melted butter

1 egg

1/4 cup fresh lemon juice

4 slices bacon

paprika

lemon wedges for garnish.

Soak fish in salt water for 5 to 10 minutes. Dry with paper towels. Mix all other ingredients except lemon juice, bacon and paprika. Stuff the fish loosely and place in a baking dish lined with aluminum foil for easy clean up. Pour lemon juice over fish. Place bacon strips on top and sprinkle with paprika. Cover with foil and bake for 1 to 1-1/4 hours at 350° or until fish flakes easily with a fork. Serve garnished with lemon wedges.
    4 servings
    Steam some mixed vegetables to add color to your table.

Pickled Northern Pike

2 cups northern fillets, cut into bite-sized chunks

3/4 cup sugar

2 tablespoons salt

2 tablespoons pickling spice

1-1/2 cups white vinegar

1/2 cup onion, sliced

Combine seasonings and vinegar in quart jar. Add fish and onions. Cover and refrigerate for five days before eating.
    Pickling is a great way to prepare small northerns because the vinegar dissolves the pesky Y-bones.

NORTHERN PIKE BAKED IN SWEET CREAM

1 3 to 4 pound northern pike, dressed, with head on

salt

flour

pepper

2 pints whipping cream

Rinse fish in cold water and then dry with paper towels. Salt lightly inside and out. Roll fish in flour to coat well, place in baking dish. Sprinkle with pepper to taste; pour on whipping cream. Bake at 350° for 1 to 1-1/2 hours or until fish flakes easily, basting every few minutes once cream has begun to boil. Stop basting during the last 15 minutes of baking to allow browning. Remove fish to a serving platter and keep warm. Boil pan juices over medium heat until thickened, stirring constantly. Pour over fish and serve.

2 servings

You'll find that boiled new potatoes go well with northern prepared this way.

EASY PICKLED FISH

4 pounds fish fillets, thinly sliced

4 cups white vinegar

1-1/2 cups sugar

3 tablespoons pickling spice

1/2 cup non-iodized salt

dill (optional)

3 large white onions, thinly sliced

Heat vinegar and add sugar to dissolve; allow to cool. Combine all ingredients except fish and onions with 4 cups cold water in a 1 gallon glass jar. Fill to top with raw fish and onions. Let stand at room temperature, lid on loosely, for 48 hours. Pour off brine leaving just enough to cover fish. Keeps in refrigerator indefinitely.

BASS IN CREAM

2 pounds bass fillets

1/2 cup flour

1 teaspoon salt

1/4 teaspoon pepper

1/4 teaspoon paprika

1 egg

1/4 cup shortening or oil

2 medium onions, sliced

1/2 cup light cream

parsley sprigs for garnish

Mix flour, salt, pepper and paprika. In another bowl, beat egg and mix with 1 tablespoon water. Dip fillets in flour mixture and then in egg mixture to coat all sides. Fry in a heavy skillet in shortening or oil until brown on one side. Turn and place onions on top of fish; continue frying until second side is brown. Drain fat. Pour cream over fish. Reduce heat, cover and simmer until cream is absorbed. Serve garnished with parsley sprigs.

6 to 8 servings

Variation: After completing frying, place fish and onions in a casserole. Pour cream over fish, cover and bake for 30 minutes at 400°.

Serve with buttered Brussels sprouts.

When I was in grade school, my family used to spend a week each summer with my cousins' families at Grandma Gert's cottage on a fantastic smallmouth lake in southern Ontario. We caught smallmouths all week and kept them in a big live box at the dock. The day before we left was fish cleaning day, and everybody helped.

We kids had the fun job. We netted the bass out of the livewell and hauled them, flopping and soaking us in slime, up the steep path to the cleaning table where Dad, Uncle Clint and Uncle Bob cleaned them. To make a game of it, we tried to see how many we could get in the net at one time.

My cousin Tom and I were struggling up the dock with a half-dozen fat smallmouths jammed in the little trout net when the biggest one — a three-pounder at least — flopped out, bounced once on the dock and gained his freedom. We expected to get chewed out by our dads, but they just laughed and said that was one less fish to clean.

On our next trip to the dock, we let two more go just to watch them swim away and never told anybody. (Dan)

BAKED BASS AU GRATIN

1 pound bass fillets

2 tablespoons fine cracker crumbs

1 cup canned tomatoes

2 tablespoons onion, chopped

1/4 teaspoon salt

1/8 teaspoon pepper

1 tablespoon butter

1/4 cup cheddar cheese, coarsely grated

Grease 1 quart shallow baking dish. Sprinkle with cracker crumbs and arrange fillets on crumbs. Combine tomatoes, onion, salt and pepper; pour over fish. Dot with butter and sprinkle with cheese. Bake for 35 minutes at 350° or until fish flakes easily.
   4 servings
   As an appetizer for this recipe, try broiled stuffed mushroom caps.

BAKED BASS WITH BACON

6 bass, dressed and scaled and cut into serving-sized portions

1/2 cup cornmeal

3/4 teaspoon salt

1 teaspoon paprika

6 slices bacon

3 tomatoes, peeled and cut into wedges

Mix cornmeal, salt and paprika. Coat both sides of fish with mixture. Place in a greased baking dish. Place bacon on top of bass. Bake for 20 minutes at 425°. Arrange tomato wedges around fish and broil 5 inches from heat for 6 minutes.
   6 servings
   You'll enjoy a side dish of au gratin potatoes with this recipe.

BLUEGILL CREAM CHEESE CASSEROLE

2 cups bluegill fillets, cut in half

1 7-ounce package macaroni

2 3-ounce packages cream cheese, softened

1 10-ounce can cream of mushroom soup

1/2 cup milk

1/2 teaspoon salt

1/8 teaspoon pepper

1/4 cup chopped green pepper

1/4 cup chopped onion

1 tablespoon prepared mustard

crushed potato chips or crackers

Prepare macaroni according to package directions. Drain. Blend cream cheese, soup and milk until smooth. Combine all ingredients, except potato chips or crackers. Pour into 2-1/2 quart casserole. Top with crumbs. Bake for 30 minutes at 350° or until bubbly and top is golden.

6 servings

This casserole may be served with green vegetables or a fresh fruit salad for a light lunch.

There is an old black and white photo in my album that shows two little girls holding up their catch for the day. We had just spent a memorable afternoon at "The Grade" near Lodi, ostensibly on a fishing trip. The cane poles and bobbers we had plied all morning had brought nothing to the surface. When Dad fired up the charcoal (originally intended to cook fish) for the hot dogs, hungry eyes looked in our direction, and we felt lucky to be alive.

In the afternoon, the one bluegill that dared to nibble at our bait provided some excitement, but I think we were equally thrilled with a clam that we found along the shore. Our total catch for the day included one bluegill, one clam, two sunburns and a whole raft of memories. My sister, Judy, and I still look at the that photo and laugh at the funny sunglasses we were wearing, and neither of us can remember who caught the fish. (Nancy)

TOMATO FRIED PERCH

2 pounds perch fillets or steaks
2 eggs
1-1/2 cups prepared biscuit mix
6 tablespoons catsup
1/2 cup shortening or oil
lemon wedges for garnish
parsley sprigs for garnish

Beat eggs and mix with 2 tablespoons water. In another bowl, blend biscuit mix and catsup. Dip perch fillets in egg mixture and then in biscuit mixture. Fry in shortening or oil until golden brown on both sides. Serve garnished with lemon wedges and parsley.
4 servings
Homemade French fries and coleslaw set off this fish fry variation.

PANFISH VEGETABLE SOUP

1 pound panfish fillets, cut into 1 inch pieces
4 slices bacon, cut up
1 medium onion, chopped
1 small green pepper, chopped
1/4 cup celery, chopped
1 clove garlic, minced
1 tablespoon plus 1 teaspoon instant chicken bouillon
1 bay leaf
1/2 teaspoon oregano
1/2 teaspoon sugar
1/4 teaspoon sage
4 tomatoes, peeled and chopped
2 cups fresh mushrooms, sliced
1 6-ounce can tomato paste
1/2 cup white wine

Cook bacon until crisp in a Dutch oven. Remove. Add onion, green pepper, celery and garlic. Sauté until tender, about 6 to 7 minutes. Return bacon to pan; add 2 cups water and all remaining ingredients except fish. Simmer for 30 minutes, stirring occasionally. Add fish. Simmer, stirring gently, until fish flakes easily, about 8 minutes.

Serve as a main course for a soup-and-sandwich lunch, or as the first course of a game dinner.

GINGER GRILLED TROUT

4 fresh trout, dressed, heads intact
3/4 teaspoon ground ginger
1/2 teaspoon cracked pepper
4 tablespoons butter
1/4 cup soy sauce
lemon wedges for garnish

Wash trout with cold water and then dry with paper towels. Cut 3 slashes into the thickest part of each side of the fish to make it cook faster and more evenly. Combine all other ingredients except lemon wedges in a small saucepan and heat until butter melts. Brush inside and outside of each trout with mixture. Place on aluminum foil in a shallow baking pan. Broil until golden brown; turn and broil other side, basting frequently, until fish flakes easily. Garnish with lemon wedges.

4 servings

Try French cut green beans with slivered almonds with this recipe.

The late Ted Trueblood, one of America's best known outdoor writers, was also quite an accomplished backwoods cook. He always prepared trout with the heads on and even ate the heads of smaller fish, often scrounging them from the plates of his camping companions.

On one fishing trip, Trueblood's partners decided to play a trick on him and served him a plateful of nothing but trout heads, while they kept the meaty portions for themselves. To their amazement and disgust, Trueblood never said a word, but ate the trout heads with gusto, bones and all.

MOLDED TROUT

6 10- to 14- inch trout
2 chicken bouillon cubes
1 tablespoon lemon juice
1 envelope unflavored gelatin
1/2 lemon, sliced thinly
10 green olives with pimiento

Cucumber Sauce Ingredients:
1/2 teaspoon salt
1/2 teaspoon parsley, chopped
1 teaspoon grated onion
3/4 cup dairy sour cream
1/4 teaspoon prepared mustard
1/2 cup cucumber, chopped
juice of 1/2 lemon

Dissolve bouillon cubes in 2 cups boiling water in a saucepan. Add lemon juice and trout. Simmer for 5 to 8 minutes. Remove trout and allow to cool. Divide along the back to make 2 fillets and remove bones. Place trout fillets on a deep serving platter. Soften gelatin in 1/4 cup cold water and add to broth in saucepan, stirring until dissolved. Refrigerate until gelatin starts to thicken. Spoon half over trout; refrigerate until firm. Top with lemon slices and olives; spoon on remaining gelatin and refrigerate until firm. Serve with cucumber sauce.

To prepare cucumber sauce, combine all ingredients in a small bowl and chill.

BASIC BROILED TROUT

trout - 1 or more per person depending on size
butter

Wash trout with cold water and dry with paper towels. Dot or brush with butter inside and out. Broil for 3 to 5 minutes on a side or until golden brown and the tail is crisp.

This is probably the world's simplest fish recipe, but it is one of the best ways to prepare fresh-caught trout. Try this when you return to camp, cabin or home after a day of stream fishing when you've caught a few trout and are too tired and hungry to prepare an elaborate meal.

STUFFED TROUT

1 medium to large trout, dressed but with head intact
2 tablespoons butter, divided
1 tablespoon chopped onion
1 tablespoon chopped celery
1 tablespoon chopped mushrooms
1-1/4 teaspoon lemon juice, divided
1/4 teaspoon sage
1/4 teaspoon oregano
1/4 teaspoon thyme
1/4 teaspoon parsley
1/4 teaspoon dill weed
salt and pepper
2/3 cup stuffing cubes

Melt 1 tablespoon butter in a deep skillet. Add onion, celery and mushrooms; sauté until tender but not soft. Add 2 tablespoons water, 1/4 teaspoon lemon juice, herbs and salt and pepper to taste. Stir in stuffing cubes. Moisten well and remove from heat. Wash trout in cold water and dry with paper towels. Place on aluminum foil. Stuff trout; baste with remaining butter and lemon juice. Wrap and double seal the foil. Bake for 30 minutes at 350°.

Variation: Use herbed stuffing cubes and omit the sage, oregano, thyme and parsley.

2 servings

Try fresh buttered green beans sprinkled with lemon and nutmeg as a side dish.

TROUT AUX POMMES

1 large trout, filleted
3 apples, cut into 1/4 inch slices
3/4 cup butter
1/4 cup honey
1/8 teaspoon garlic salt
1 teaspoon pepper
1/8 teaspoon celery salt
1/8 teaspoon basil
1/8 teaspoon tarragon
1 teaspoon paprika
3/4 teaspoon cayenne
1/8 teaspoon grated lemon rind

Arrange apple slices on foil-lined cookie sheet. Melt butter and honey together in a small saucepan; stir in all other seasonings. Brush sauce on both sides of trout; place on apple slices, skin-side up. Broil 8 to 10 inches from heat for 3 to 7 minutes or until skin bubbles. Lower heat to 400°. Turn fish and brush with sauce. Bake 10 minutes per inch of fillet thickness or until fish flakes easily.

2 servings

BAKED TROUT WITH LEMON AND MUSHROOMS

1 medium to large trout, dressed but with head intact

1/2 tablespoon chopped parsley

1/8 teaspoon nutmeg

2/3 cup sliced mushrooms

1/3 cup melted butter

juice of 1/2 lemon

paprika

Wash trout with cold water and dry with paper towels. Place fish in a baking dish. Combine parsley, nutmeg, mushrooms, melted butter and lemon juice. Pour over fish. Sprinkle with paprika and bake for 25 to 30 minutes at 350°.

2 servings

To serve your guests a springtime meal you've gathered yourself (and one they'll rave about), prepare a fresh-caught steelhead using this recipe and serve it with steamed wild asparagus and homemade hollandaise sauce, topped off by a wild greens salad of sorrel, lamb's-quarters and mint from your favorite foraging ground.

My brother Mike and my cousins Tom and Doug and I were just picking at the pink-fleshed brook trout on our plates when one of my uncles asked what was wrong.

"This fish tastes awful," we said.

He tried a piece and pronounced it delicious. "You'll never get fresher fish," he told us. "We just caught these brookies this morning."

"No!" we told him. "Put a piece of fish in your mouth and then drink some milk. It's yucky! It's poison!"

He obliged us and practically gagged. Gleefully, we all shouted, "See!"

"Yeah, I see," he replied when he could catch his breath. "The milk's sour!" (Dan)

TROUT WITH RICE STUFFING

2 whole trout, dressed

4 slices bacon

1/4 cup long grain rice

1 envelope chicken bouillon

2 tablespoons green onions, chopped

2 tablespoons lemon juice

Rinse trout in cold water, dry with paper towels and set aside. Cook bacon until golden (but not browned) in a medium-sized skillet; remove. Cook rice for one minute in bacon drippings, add 2/3 cup water and bouillon and heat to boiling. Cover and cook over low heat for 15 minutes or until tender and all liquid is absorbed. Add green onions, stir and remove from heat. Sprinkle cavity of trout with lemon juice, stuff with rice and secure with toothpicks. Wrap each trout in 2 slices of bacon, place in a baking dish and bake for 20 minutes at 350° or until fish flakes easily.

2 servings

A ginger and lemon dressing on a fresh green salad gives this meal an oriental flavor.

SALMON ON THE GRILL

1 salmon, cut into steaks

2 teaspoons oregano

1 teaspoon garlic powder

salt and pepper to taste

1 small onion, thinly sliced

1 tablespoon plus 1 teaspoon soy sauce

2 ounces salad oil

2 ounces lemon juice

Mix all ingredients except salmon. Place steaks in a shallow pan and pour sauce over them. Turn to coat both sides. Let stand for 30 minutes. Place steaks on heavy duty aluminum foil, fold front and back edges together to seal, fold in sides. Place on rack over hot coals or in a 400° oven and bake for 10 minutes. Open carefully to release steam without spilling the juices. Baste with sauce. Continue cooking with foil open until salmon flakes easily, basting frequently.

3 to 4 servings

Bake potatoes in aluminum foil on the coals while you grill your salmon.

SALLY'S SALMON DILL BAKE

1 large salmon or trout fillet, skin removed

1 cup mayonnaise

1 teaspoon dill weed

3/4 teaspoon garlic powder

Place fillet in shallow baking pan.

Mix mayonnaise, dill and garlic powder and spread evenly over fillet, sealing it to the pan. Bake at 350° for 35 minutes or until mayonnaise is golden brown.

2 to 3 servings

GRILLED SALMON STEAKS WITH HERB BUTTER

4 salmon steaks, 3/4 to 1 inch thick

3 tablespoons butter, melted

1 tablespoon peanut or vegetable oil

Herb Butter Ingredients:

2 tablespoons basil

1 tablespoon tarragon

1 tablespoon minced chives

freshly ground pepper to taste

3 ounces butter, softened

1 tablespoon fresh lemon juice

To prepare the herb butter, cream the butter in a large bowl until smooth and soft. Add basil, tarragon and chives; mix well. Add lemon juice and pepper and mix again. Shape into a cylinder about 1 inch in diameter. Wrap with foil or plastic wrap. Chill in the refrigerator for 1 to 2 hours or for 30 minutes in the freezer.

Mix melted butter and oil; brush on steaks. Grill about 6 inches from the heat for about 6 minutes on the first side, 4 minutes on the second side, basting occasionally. Serve topped with a pat of herb butter.

4 servings

Serve with twice-baked potatoes and a fresh green salad for a healthful and delicious meal.

CAPTAIN DARRELL'S SALMON SUPREME

4 fresh salmon or trout fillets (about 2 pounds) cut into serving-
    sized pieces

4 tablespoons oregano

1-1/2 cups flour

salt and pepper

2 tablespoons butter

1 large onion, sliced

10 - 12 mushrooms, sliced

juice of 1/2 lemon

1/2 cup sweet vermouth

Mix oregano and flour. Season with salt and pepper. Lightly flour each fillet. Sauté onions and mushrooms in butter in a frying pan. Move them to the side while you brown the fillets. Sprinkle extra oregano and lemon juice over fish.

When almost done increase heat, add vermouth and sear all ingredients, turning fish several times and stirring vegetables. Serve on rice. This recipe gives salmon a nutty taste. Even people who don't like fish love this one.

4 servings

CAJUN SALMON

1 salmon, filleted, skin on, cut
    into serving-sized pieces

1 teaspoon salt

1 tablespoon seasoned salt

1 teaspoon onion salt

1/2 teaspoon onion powder

1 teaspoon garlic powder

1 teaspoon black pepper

1/2 teaspoon white pepper

1/2 teaspoon cayenne

1/4 teaspoon paprika

1/4 teaspoon parsley flakes

1/2 teaspoon celery seed

1 onion, sliced, split into rings

1 10-ounce can pitted black
    olives, cut in half

8 ounces mozzarella cheese,
    grated

Place the fish pieces skin-side down on individual sheets of heavy duty aluminum foil. Combine all spices and mix well. Sprinkle liberally over fish. Top with onion rings, olive halves and cheese. Fold the front and back of the foil together to make a tight seal, folding the ends in tightly. Cook for 20 to 25 minutes over open coals on the grill. Do not open foil during cooking time or fish may dry out.

3 to 4 servings

Serve with steamed okra and hot biscuits.

SALMON WITH WATERCRESS-SPINACH SAUCE

2 pounds salmon fillets

1 bunch watercress

1 pound spinach

2 tablespoons butter

1 cup dry white wine

2 tablespoons chopped chives

2 tablespoons tarragon

salt and pepper

1/2 cup dairy sour cream

Remove the stems from the watercress and spinach; discard. Wash the leaves and shake off excess water; set aside. Sauté salmon in butter until it is cooked through, but still firm. Place on a serving dish and keep warm. Add wine to the cooking juices and mix well, blending in all bits. Add watercress, spinach, chives, tarragon and salt and pepper to taste. Cook for 2 minutes or until leaves are soft. Purée in blender. Return to the pan and bring to a boil. Add sour cream and return to a boil, stirring constantly. Remove from heat immediately and pour sauce over salmon for serving.

Variation: Substitute 1 cup fish stock for the cup of wine.

4 servings

Serve with stewed tomatoes on the side and a loaf of homemade bread.

SMOKED SALMON QUICHE

1 cup smoked salmon, cut into small pieces

4 eggs

1 can evaporated milk or heavy cream

1 teaspoon onion powder or 1/2 medium onion, finely chopped

1 teaspoon garlic powder (optional)

salt and pepper

1 pie crust shell, frozen and thawed or homemade

1 cup grated Swiss cheese, divided

1/2 cup part-skim mozzarella cheese, divided

1/2 cup grated cheddar cheese

1/4 cup fresh chives, chopped

Beat eggs. Add milk, onion powder, garlic powder, salt and pepper to taste. Mix well; set aside. Place pie crust in baking dish. Layer with half of the Swiss cheese, half of the mozzarella, the salmon, remaining Swiss and remaining mozzarella. Pour on milk/egg mixture. Sprinkle on cheddar cheese and chives. Bake at 350° for 45 to 50 minutes or until golden brown. Let cook about 15 minutes before cutting. Good either warm or cold.

4 to 6 servings

Variation: For those on a low fat diet, omit from the above recipe:

omit	and replace with:
4 eggs	2 whole eggs plus 2 egg whites
1 can evaporated milk or heavy cream	1 can evaporated milk
1 cup Swiss cheese	1/2 cup grated Swiss cheese
1/2 cup mozzarella cheese	1-1/4 cup grated mozzarella cheese
1/2 cup Cheddar cheese	1/4 cup grated cheddar cheese

MANHATTAN FISH STEW

2 pounds fish fillets, cut into bite-sized chunks

1 medium chopped onion

1 tablespoon vegetable oil

1 28-ounce can tomatoes, undrained

1 teaspoon salt

1/2 teaspoon basil

1/4 teaspoon sugar

2 medium potatoes, peeled and diced

1 10-ounce package frozen corn

Sauté onion in oil until tender in a 4-quart saucepan. Stir in tomatoes with liquid, potatoes, salt, basil and sugar. Heat to boiling. Reduce heat, cover and simmer for 20 minutes, stirring occasionally. Add fish and corn and return to boil. Reduce heat, cover and simmer for 5 minutes or until fish flakes easily and vegetables are tender.

4 to 6 servings

Bring this stew along in a wide-mouth thermos for a hot lunch on a winter outing.

I've heard many people say it, but I don't think you can appreciate the truth in the statement until you've experienced it yourself. Fishing is not simply catching fish. Fishing can be the day, the weather, your fishing companions, and yes, fish can make it more rewarding, but it can be other things, too. It can be the leopard frogs you saw by the dock, learning how the lily pads grow, or a conversation with a special person that you wouldn't have had if you hadn't been fishing. Fishing can be a kick-back sort of day where nothing really matters, or it can be an experience in earnest, knowing that your catch will make the difference between a meal and a snack. (Nancy)

We really only did two kinds of fishing when I was young, and I think I preferred drop-line fishing to bobbers. I had a stronger sense of connection between me and the fish. When they nibbled, I could feel it directly through the line I held in my hand. I didn't have to wait for the red and white plastic ball to bob a little faster than usual or for my eyes to tell my brain to tell my hand to respond. I knew I had a bite—RIGHT NOW!

Drop lines also gave me the luxury of leaning back against the thwart of our big canoe, padded by my life preserver from my position in the bottom of the boat, and tipping my head back to soak up some of the warm summer sunshine. I could listen to the birdcalls and the breezes playing in the trees on shore, as the water gently lapped at the gunwales. (Nancy)

FRIED CATFISH WITH PINEAPPLE SAUCE

2 pounds catfish fillets, skinned

soy sauce

1 cup flour

salt and pepper

2 tablespoons vegetable oil

1 20-ounce can pineapple tidbits, undrained

2 tablespoons cornstarch

2 cups cooked rice

Cut catfish fillets into serving-sized pieces and marinate in soy sauce for 45 minutes. Season flour with salt and pepper. Dredge catfish in flour and fry in hot oil until golden brown.

To make sauce, pour pineapple tidbits into saucepan and heat to boiling, stirring occasionally. Dissolve 2 tablespoons cornstarch in 1/3 cup cold water. Turn heat down to simmer and slowly add dissolved cornstarch, stirring constantly until mixture thickens. Place fried catfish pieces on bed of rice and pour sauce over fish.

4 servings

CATFISH WITH VEGETABLES

4 catfish fillets

2 tablespoons butter

2 carrots, cut in thin strips

2 stalks diced celery

2 tablespoons chopped parsley

1 turnip, cut in thin strips

1 onion, thinly sliced

salt and pepper

4 cups white wine or chicken broth

1 teaspoon cornstarch in 2 tablespoons water

Sauté vegetables in butter over low heat until soft. Season with salt and pepper to taste. Pour wine into a saucepan, add fish and bring to a boil. Simmer for 10 to 15 minutes until catfish is cooked. Remove fish to a heated serving platter. Boil the wine until it is reduced by half and thicken with dissolved cornstarch. Add vegetables. Pour over fish and serve over toast.

4 servings

For a southern flavor, cook up some hush puppies!

BAKED SHEEPSHEAD IN TOMATO DILL SAUCE

1 pound sheepshead fillets, brown streak along sides removed

1 cup chopped onion

2 tablespoons butter

1 tablespoon flour

1 10-ounce can condensed consommé, undiluted

1/2 cup tomato catsup

3/4 dill chopped pickle

Sauté onions in butter. Stir in flour; gradually add consommé and catsup. Simmer for 25 minutes, stirring occasionally. Add pickles. Place fish in baking dish and pour sauce over. Bake 25 to 30 minutes at 400° or until fish flakes easily with a fork.

4 servings

Serve with boiled diced potatoes, fried and garnished with paprika.

When we first taste a finished recipe on the air, we are prepared to say, "Oh...that tastes good!" or something similar. Looking at the ingredients for this recipe, we thought we might have to do a little acting to come up with a positive line, but it surprised us. I think you could hear our true feelings in our comment that was more like "This IS good!" (Nancy)

DRUM (SHEEPSHEAD) CHOWDER

1 pound drum fillets cut into 1/2 inch cubes

1/4 cup butter

1 cup onion, thinly sliced

1 cup sliced carrots

3 medium potatoes, diced

2 tablespoons salt

1/8 teaspoon pepper

3 cups milk

1/2 teaspoon rosemary

1/4 teaspoon thyme

salt and pepper

2 tablespoons flour

1 cup light cream

Melt butter in a large saucepan, adding onion, carrots, potato, 1 cup water, salt and pepper. Cover and simmer about 15 to 20 minutes or until carrots are tender. Add fish, milk, herbs and additional salt to taste. Heat to simmering and cook until fish flakes easily. Blend flour and cream. Add to chowder and heat thoroughly.

Yield: about 8 cups

A grilled cheese and onion sandwich would go well with a steaming bowl of chowder.

Many viewers who sent us sheepshead recipes also told us about the lucky "stones" found in sheepsheads' heads. You're supposed to dig them out, dry them and carry them for good luck, sort of like aquatic rabbit's feet.

We tried the recipes, but we're not quite ready to dig bones out of fish heads and carry them around in our pockets. Besides, maybe the "luck" they bring is the kind that helps you catch more sheepshead. Now if walleyes had stones in their heads . . . . (Dan)

Poor man's Shrimp Cocktail

sheepshead fillets, cut into 1 inch strips

salt

lettuce leaves

celery, cut into chunks

fresh lemon juice

catsup

horseradish

Slice sheepshead fillets into 1 inch strips. Drop into boiling salted water. Boil 2 minutes, remove and drain. Refrigerate for 4 hours. To prepare individual salad bowls, arrange several lettuce leaves in each; add celery chunks, then sheepshead strips. Sprinkle with lemon juice and cover with a seafood cocktail sauce of catsup and horseradish mixed to your taste.

Oven Fried Sheepshead

1 3- to 4- pound sheepshead, filleted, skinned, brown stripe
    removed from the skin side of fillet

3/4 cup cornflake crumbs

1/2 cup crushed crackers

1/4 teaspoon salt

1/2 teaspoon pepper

1/2 teaspoon basil

1 teaspoon lemon juice

Mix 1 teaspoon salt per cup of water to cover fillets. Soak fillets in salted water overnight. Rinse in cold water and dry with a paper towel. Combine cornflake crumbs, crushed cracker, salt, pepper and basil. Roll fillets in mixture to coat well; place on a non-stick pan. Sprinkle with lemon juice. Bake for 12 to 20 minutes at 375° or until fish flakes easily with a fork.

  2 to 3 servings
Serve cottage fries and a green vegetable with this recipe.

WILD EDIBLES

Collecting wild edible plants is an exciting thing to do. It allows you to spend some time outdoors, appreciate the bounty that the earth provides for us and learn, at a very basic level, something about each individual plant that you collect. One of the nice things about collecting wild plants is that it's done in the spring, summer or fall of the year, all nice seasons to be out.

In order to feel successful with wild plants you have to be open to new sensations in flavor, willing to put in some extra time to carefully identify and to selectively collect the plants. You want to be sure to take only a portion of what is available in any given area in order to leave a growing stock for future seasons. Most field guides have either photographs or drawings as well as detailed descriptions of the plant to help you, so we have dispensed with that information for this chapter.

The recipes included in this chapter are straightforward and easy to follow. We like simplicity in preparation and in flavor with most wild edibles. We hope you enjoy them as much as we do.

CATTAILS

During much of the year, the cattail provides wild food for us, and knowing when to collect which parts is not difficult. Collection dates may vary considerably, being somewhat later in the north. Keeping an eye on plants in a local pond or wetland will give you a good idea of when they will be ready for your table. Since all cattails don't bloom at the same time, collection at the various stages may extend up to six weeks.

EARLY SEASON - APRIL AND MAY

Cattail Shoots - *When the plants are about two feet high and the marsh is just starting to green, the inner leaves can be slipped out and the white portion of the leaves chopped into two-inch lengths. If you want the most tender shoot, unwrap the leaves to reveal the round central core. These parts can be eaten raw, or they may be cooked in a little salted water and served with butter, but I think they are tastier cooked with a stew or roast.*

MAY AND JUNE

Spikes - *The green bloom spikes must be gathered before the pollen develops, so they are cut from the stalk while still enveloped in their papery sheath. The husk is removed before cooking and, like corn, the spikes are best cooked soon after collection. These spikes are prepared as corn-on-the-cob would be, and taste best smothered in butter. The kernels tend to be a little dry in texture. They may be eaten from the "cob" which is a hard whitish spike. These must be eaten hot to give the best flavor, so we serve them at the table in their boiling water. If you prefer not to nibble buds from the spikes at the table, you can remove them from the spikes before cooking.*

JUNE

Cattail Pollen - *Cattail pollen can be easily collected by bending the yellow flower heads into a bucket and brushing pollen off with your hand. Sift the pollen through a sieve and you are ready for cattail muffins or pancakes.*

OCTOBER AND NOVEMBER (Only for the hardy collector: Get your feet wet now?)

Cattail Roots - *The sprouts leading off the main root can be peeled and boiled. They have a slightly sweet taste and can be served with butter or cooked with meat. There is a sizeable lump of starchy material nearest the main root which can be placed in your roaster with meat.*

CATTAIL MUFFINS

3/4 cup cattail pollen
1 cup white flour
1/4 cup sugar
2-1/2 teaspoons baking powder

3/4 teaspoon salt
1 egg, well beaten
3/4 cup milk
1/3 cup vegetable oil

Sift dry ingredients into bowl and make a well in the center. Combine egg, milk and oil. Add to dry ingredients and mix only until moist. Fill greased muffin tins 2/3 full and bake at 400° for 20 to 25 minutes.
Yeild: 10 muffins

CATTAIL PANCAKES

3/4 cup cattail pollen
3/4 cup white flour
3 teaspoons baking powder
1 tablespoon sugar
1/2 teaspoon salt

1 egg, beaten
1 cup milk
2 tablespoons vegetable oil or
   melted bacon fat

Stir together dry ingredients. Combine egg, milk and oil or fat. Stir into dry ingredients until moistened. Bake on hot griddle.
Yeild: 8 small pancakes

ROAST WITH CATTAIL SHOOTS

1-1/2 pound chuck roast or
   venison roast
salt
pepper
flour
2 tablespoons vegetable oil

1 onion, sliced
4 large carrots
4 potatoes cut in 1-1/2 inch cubes
2-1/2 cups cattail shoots

Lightly salt and pepper roast on both sides; roll in flour and brown in oil about 7 minutes on each side. Add 1-1/2 cups water to pan. Spread onion slices over roast, reduce heat and simmer for 1 hour. Add vegetables water if needed, and simmer 1 hour.

Duck Potato Salad

1 quart duck potatoes, boiled, then peeled

4 hard-boiled eggs, diced

1/4 cup onion, diced

1/3 cup celery, diced

1 cup mayonnaise

Mix all ingredients and place on a fresh lettuce leaf — and enjoy!

One of the foods my sister introduced us to is the duck potato — the common name for the arrowhead root. The botanical name for the arrowhead plant is Sagittarian, which means arrowhead. Arrowhead is an aquatic plant that is very common and is found virtually everywhere in the United States, as well as some places in Canada and Mexico. It prefers to keep its feet wet in the oozy mud bordering ponds, streams and swamps, which makes it a challenge for the collector. You'll recognize the arrow-shaped leaves held about a foot above the water on a graceful stem. During the summer, they give rise to a delicate spray of small flowers.

The best time to collect the tubers is late fall before the water skims over with ice. Of course, your diagnostic leaves are gone, but if you've marked your arrowhead patch either by hand or landmark, the roots and tubers will wait there for you. The largest may be the size of a small egg, the smallest hardly noticeable. The average size is 3/4-inch to 1-inch in diameter.

The Indians used to collect them by walking barefoot and pulling out the roots with their toes. A better method is to use a long-handled garden claw. You can pull up the roots in small areas and collect the tubers as they float on the water. Arrowhead often grows thickly and your collecting actually thins the plants and allows next year's crop to produce a higher yield. It would be difficult for you to collect an entire colony, but please, take only what you need and collect lightly from a larger area rather than concentrating on a small spot.

The consistency of the prepared root tubers resembles the firm starchiness of a potato, but there is an added flavor. You will find this flavor any way you prepare the roots. You can use them as you would potatoes in recipes calling for cream sauces, or boiled new potatoes, but my introduction to them was in Duck Potato Salad, which was excellent. (Nancy)

CREAM OF MILKWEED SOUP

3 cups chopped milkweed plant (Asclepias syriaca) tops and flower
  buds, best picked in June and early July

1/2 cup chopped onion

2 stalks celery, chopped

2 tablespoons butter

3 packages (.13 oz. each) G. Washington's Golden Seasoning

1 can cream of celery soup

1/2 soup can milk

Parboil milkweed in two changes of water. Drain. Sauté onion and celery in butter. Add 1-1/2 cups water and Golden Seasoning. Stir well. Add milkweed, bring to a boil and simmer for 30 minutes. Add cream of celery soup and milk. Stir well. Heat until hot but do not boil.

CREAMED WILD LEEK SOUP

2 cups fresh chopped wild leek leaves

2 slices thick cut bacon

2 tablespoons flour

3 cups water

1-2/3 cups condensed milk

1 teaspoon salt

1/8 teaspoon black pepper

Wild leek (Allium tricoccum) is a harbinger of spring in Wisconsin. It can be found in rich wet woods and along river or stream banks in April. Gather the first leaves.

Fry bacon in a pan until crisp. Remove, cool and crumble into small pieces and return to the pan. Add flour to the bacon and drippings to make a paste. Brown slowly. Add 3 cups water, milk, salt and pepper. Cook and stir over low heat until thickened. Add leek leaves and let simmer for about 20 minutes, stirring constantly to prevent scorching and curdling.

The soup tastes best when cooled and later reheated, allowing the wild leek flavor to draw through. It can be frozen for up to three months with little loss of flavor.

HIGHBUSH CRANBERRY JUICE

4 quarts ripe highbush cranberries

juice and grated peel of one orange

sugar or honey to taste

Crush 4 quarts of berries in a large pot and add enough water to cover. Add orange juice and peel and simmer for about 5 minutes, stirring constantly. Strain through cheesecloth to remove pulp and seeds, then heat the juice to boiling. Dilute with two parts water to one part juice and sweeten to taste with sugar or honey to make a delicious wild fruit drink.

HIGHBUSH CRANBERRY JELLY

4 cups undiluted highbush cranberry juice

1 package powdered pectin

4 cups sugar

Prepare juice as in recipe for highbush cranberry juice, without adding water, then let settle in a large bowl for 4 to 8 hours. Pour off 4 cups of juice into a saucepan, stir in pectin and bring to a boil. Stir in sugar and heat again to boiling. Boil for 1 minute, then pour into jars and seal.

Tart and full-bodied, highbush cranberry jelly makes an excellent accompaniment to wild game dinners or may be used as a spread for toast and biscuits.

FRIED CLOVER BLOSSOMS

4 cups clover blossoms, moistened

1/2 cup flour

1/4 cup water

1/4 teaspoon salt

1/8 teaspoon pepper

vegetable oil for frying

Make a batter of the flour and water. Season to taste. Dip blossoms in batter and drop into pan with hot vegetable oil. Turn until batter is browned on all sides.

You can improve the batter with other spices like garlic or onion powder, but we prefer to taste the clover.

These may be served as an accompaniment to a lunch or dinner as you would serve potato chips, or as an appetizer.

FRIED QUEEN ANNE'S LACE

2 to 3 dozen medium to large opened blossoms

1-1/3 cup flour

1 teaspoon salt

1/4 teaspoon pepper

1 tablespoon vegetable oil

2 eggs

3/4 cup flat beer (or milk)

vegetable oil for frying

Wash blossoms and shake dry. Cut each stem to 8 to 10 inches. Combine all other ingredients except beer and mix well. Gently add beer or milk. Allow batter to rest in the refrigerator for at least 3 hours.

Dip blossoms in batter. Allow to drip, head down, onto waxed paper for at least 1/2 hour. Cut stems and drop into heated cooking oil. Deep fry to golden brown. Drain and serve.

ROADSIDE DELIGHT TOSSED SALAD

Redroot or pigweed (*Amaranthus retroflexus*) *For a real taste of spinach, pick the young terminal leaves.*

Lamb's quarters (*Chenopodium album*) *For an endive-like flavor, use the young terminal leaves.*

Purslane (*Portulaca oleracea*) *Use the stems and leaves for a crispy, watery texture.*

Red clover (*Trifolium pratense*) *Use the new, fresh blooming flower heads for a sweet nectar taste.*

Common chickweed (*Stellaria media*) *Use fresh leaf and stem material for an astringent iron taste.*

Wood sorrel (*Oxalis stricta*) *Use fresh stem and leaf material for a tart and tangy flavor.*

Penny cress (*Thlaspi arvense*) *Use green stem and leaves which are spicy bitter, or dry seeds like black pepper.*

Shepherd's purse (*Capsella bursa-pastoris*) *Use green stem and leaf, or fruit parts for a tangy, peppery flavor.*

Optional Substitutions:

Sheep sorrel (*Rumex acetosella*) *for a rhubarb-like tartness, or pepper grass (lepidium campestre) for a spicy, tangy flavor.*

Harvest fresh greens and flower parts. Rinse gently and let soak in cold water for 15 to 20 minutes. Drain in a colander and chill in the refrigerator. Chop and toss equal amounts into a salad mix.

Serve with a light vinegar and oil dressing to avoid masking the flavors.

This delightful combination of wild salad ingredients is rich in vitamins and minerals, low in calories, a flavor exercise for daring taste buds. It also leaves a pleasing aftertaste on the palate.

SEASONED MOREL SAUTÉ

2 pounds fresh morel mushrooms
1/2 cup butter
1/2 cup chopped onions
1 teaspoon oregano or thyme
1 teaspoon salt
1/4 teaspoon pepper
2 tablespoons Worcestershire sauce

Clean the morels and cut in half lengthwise. Sauté onions in butter for two minutes. Add morels, oregano or thyme, salt and pepper. Cook and stir for two additional minutes. Add Worcestershire; turn off the heat, cover and let stand to absorb the flavorings. Reheat, if necessary, prior to serving.

DANDELION BUDS

dandelion buds
butter
salt

Place dandelion buds in a sauce pan and add enough boiling water to cover. Cover pan and set on low burner for three minutes. Drain and season with butter and salt.

DANDELION COFFEE

In a field where you find large dandelions, dig the large forked roots. Clean and place on a cookie sheet. Roast slowly at 325° for 4 hours, or until the roots break with a snap and are dark brown in the center. Grind the roots and use as you would regular coffee, only a little less in amount.

RECIPE CONTRIBUTORS

George & Myrtle Alderson

Darrell Baker

Patrick Barwick

Ann Beck

Jim Brakken

John & Carol Brennan

Steve & Molly Duren

Denny & Deb Egan

Ken Engman

Irene Farrenkopf

Angelo Fraboni

Charlie & Vivian France

Peter Fredricksen

Hilary Anne Frost-Kumpf

Michele Geslin-Small

Julie Henrichs

Joyce Herriges

Reed J. Huenink

Margy Huettner

Lewis James

Lorie Kaminski

Linda Krakow

Leigh L. LIndow

Michelle Love

Randy Lunde

Tom & Martha Merten

LaDonna P. Morse

Nancy Muraszewski

Joy Nolan

Amy P. Pauers

Al Pipke

Betty Pouros

Randy Powers

Dave & Barb Sarnowski

Jonathon Small

Gene & Bess Small

Alice Tesch

Kathy Tranchita

"Skinny" Walters

Ilona Willing

Petra Wood

Mike Zaffke